W9-DEE-807

Many Gifts

Theological Advisor
Fr. Michael T. Ryan

Series Authors
Mary Cairo
Luci Soncin

Series Consultant
Jennette MacKenzie

Social Studies Consultant
Angelo Bolotta

Assessment Consultant
Fran Craig

St. Francis Xavier Elementary School
111 Bartley Bull Parkway
Brampton, Ontario
L6W 2J8

 NELSON EDUCATION

NELSON EDUCATION

Many Gifts 3 Student Book

Theological Advisor
Fr. Michael T. Ryan

Series Consultant
Jennette MacKenzie

Series Authors
Mary Cairo
Luci Soncin

Social Studies Consultant
Angelo Bolotta

Executive Publisher
Lara Caplan

Managing Editor
Alexandra Romic

Senior Editor
Diane Robitaille

Product Manager
Jessie MacKinnon

Program Manager
Kim Toffan

Developmental Editors
Natalia Diaz
Margaret Hoogeveen

Editorial Assistant
Megan Watcher

Researcher
Rachel Horner

Fact Checkers
Fraser Los
Tracy Westell

Director, Content and Media Production
Linh Vu

Senior Production Project Manager
Jane High

Senior Content Production Editor
Jane High

Copyeditor
Linda Szostak

Proofreader
Paula Pettitt-Townsend

Indexer
Belle Wong

Design Director
Ken Phipps

Interior Design
Jennifer Leung
Trinh Truong

Cover Design
Jennifer Leung
Trinh Truong

Cover Images
(central image) © Mary Ellen McQuay/First Light; (bottom left) *View of the Market Place and Catholic Church, Uppertown, Québec–1832*, Robert Auchmuty Sproule, 1874, M6981, McCord Museum, Montréal; (bottom centre) Library and Archives Canada, Acc. No. 1970-188-1090 W.H. Coverdale Collection of Canadiana; (bottom right) *Indians transporting furs through the Canadian wilderness, 1858* (oil on canvas), Krieghoff, Cornelius (1815–72)/Hudson Bay Company, Canada/Bridgeman Images

Asset Coordinator
Suzanne Peden

Illustrators
Jamel Akib
Ellen Beier
Julia Bereciartu
Michael Borop
Crowle Art
Valentina Jaskina
John Mantha
Kelley McMorris
Craig Orback
Karelyn Siegler
Kim Smith
Laszlo Veres
Lin Wang

Compositors
Barb Kelly
Jennifer Leung
Kathy Mo

Photo/Permissions Researcher
Eva Svec

COPYRIGHT © 2015 by
Nelson Education Ltd.

ISBN-13: 978-0-17-653053-2
ISBN-10: 0-17-653053-3

Printed and bound in Canada
3 4 5 6 19 18 17 16

For more information contact Nelson Education Ltd., 1120 Birchmount Road, Toronto, Ontario M1K 5G4. Or you can visit our website at www.nelson.com.

Excerpts from this publication may be reproduced under licence from Access Copyright, or with the express written permission of Nelson Education Ltd., or as permitted by law. Requests which fall outside of Access Copyright guidelines must be submitted online to www.cengage.com/permissions. Further questions about permissions can be emailed to permissionrequest@cengage.com.

ALL RIGHTS ARE OTHERWISE RESERVED. No part of this publication may be reproduced, stored in a retrieval system, or transmitted in any form or by any means, electronic, mechanic, photocopying, scanning, recording or otherwise, except as specifically authorized.

Every effort has been made to trace ownership of all copyrighted material and to secure permission from copyright holders. In the event of any question arising as to the use of any material, we will be pleased to make the necessary corrections in future printings.

Advisory Panel

Patricia Amos
Michael Bator
Fran Craig
Martha Dutrizak
Aimee Gerdevich
Anne Jamieson
Lorne Keon
Bronek Korczynski
John Kostoff
Dr. Josephine Lombardi
Patricia Manson
Noel Martin
Sharron McKeever
Jim Minello
Susan Perry
Lou Rocha
Suzanne Wishak

Nelson Education would like to offer special thanks to Sr. Joan Cronin, g.s.i.c., for her guidance and advice.

Series Consultants and Contributors

Mary Bender, Assessment Contributor
Dr. Henry V. Bishop, African
   Heritage Reviewer
Michael Borop, Cartography Reviewer
Wilfred Burton, Aboriginal Reviewer
Nancy Christoffer, Bias and Equity Reviewer
Lynnita-Jo Guillet, Aboriginal Reviewer
Stanley Hallman-Chong, Curriculum Expert
Tanya Leary, Aboriginal Reviewer
Paula Markus, Bias and Equity Reviewer
Professor Ovey Mohammed, s.j.,
   Theology Reviewer
Byron Moldofsky, Cartography Reviewer
Dyanne Rivers, Social Studies Reviewer
Dr. Pamela Toulouse, Aboriginal Reviewer
Professor Rachel Urowitz, Religious
   History Reviewer

Series Reviewers

Antoinette Armenti-Lambert, *Niagara CDSB*
Christine Battagli, *Niagara CDSB*
Mariella Bruni, *Dufferin–Peel CDSB*
Betty Brush, *Windsor–Essex CDSB*
Lori Bryden, *Algonquin and Lakeshore CDSB*
Michelle Bryden, *CDSB of Eastern Ontario*
Monica Campbell, *London DCSB*
Erin Cassone, *Huron–Perth CDSB*
Alan Creelman, *Niagara CDSB*
Nancy Das Neves, *Toronto CDSB*
Marina DiGirolamo, *York CDSB*
Shawn Evon, *Dufferin–Peel CDSB*
Vania Grober*, Toronto CDSB*
Anna Harris, *Thunder Bay CDSB*
Julia Janveau, *Nipissing–Parry Sound CDSB*
Deborah Karam, *Toronto CDSB*
Vivian Ku, *York CDSB*
Isabel Machado, *Algonquin and Lakeshore CDSB*
Anne Marie Maloney, *Niagara CDSB*
Debbie Matthews, *Peterborough Victoria
   Northumberland and Clarington CDSB*
Veronica McCarren, *Simcoe Muskoka CDSB*
Suzanne McLaughlin, *Windsor–Essex CDSB*
Yvonne Minard, *Durham CDSB*
Susan Nelan, *Hamilton–Wentworth CDSB*
Susanne Nolan, *Nipissing–Parry Sound CDSB*
Terri Pauco, *Niagara CDSB*
Michelle Peres, *Toronto CDSB*
Deanna Perry, *Ottawa CSB*
Ralph Peter, *Toronto CDSB*
Lino Pin, *Hamilton–Wentworth CDSB*
Carmelina Pinozzotto, *Niagara CDSB*
Grant Ranalli, *Hamilton–Wentworth CDSB*
Daniel Reidy, *Dufferin–Peel CDSB*
Lynne Ruetz, *Durham CDSB*
Sandra Scime, *Hamilton–Wentworth CDSB*
Alan Skeoch, Retired, *Toronto DSB*
Jillian Stefik, *Durham CDSB*
Seán Stokes, *St. Michael's College School*
William Swartz, Retired, *Toronto DSB*
David Tignanelli, *Nipissing–Parry Sound CDSB*
Carol Vaage, *Edmonton CS*
Josie Zuppa, *Hamilton–Wentworth CDSB*

Contributing Writers

Tara Harte
Douglas Paton

Contents Many Gifts 3

Unit 2 Early Communities in Canada

Why Do You Learn Social Studies?

You learn social studies to become a better member of your community. Learning about Canada and the world helps you become a responsible, active citizen. This diagram shows what being an active citizen means.

Active Participation

This means working for the common good in your community.

Identity

This means understanding who you are and what different communities you belong to.

Structures

This means understanding how communities are organized.

Attributes

This means demonstrating positive character traits, such as responsibility and respect.

What Are You Going to Learn?

This resource is divided into two units. The first unit is called **Living and Working in Ontario**. In this unit, you will learn about the different landform regions of Ontario. You will explore the connections between landform features and how people live and work. You will also explore the effects of human activities on God's Creation.

The second unit is called **Early Communities in Canada**. In this unit, you will learn about different communities in Canada between 1780 and 1850. You will explore how people lived and the challenges they faced. As well, you will compare how people lived in the past with how people live today.

How Are You Going to Learn?

The inquiry process can help you investigate topics. It can also help you solve problems and draw conclusions. The inquiry process has five parts, as shown in the diagram at the right.

You may not use all of the parts of the inquiry process during every investigation. Sometimes, you will use the same parts more than once.

The Inquiry Process

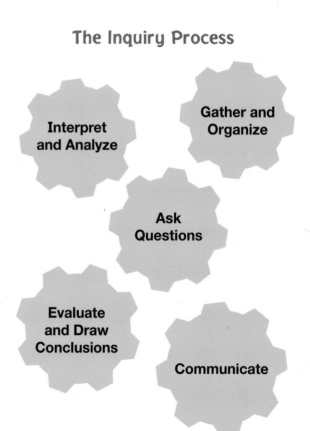

Interpret and Analyze

Gather and Organize

Ask Questions

Evaluate and Draw Conclusions

Communicate

Social Studies Thinking Concepts

These **thinking concepts** give you ways to look at and understand information when learning about social studies.

When You Think about ...	You Might Ask Yourself ...
Significance	• What is significant? • Who is it significant to? • Why is it significant?
Cause and Consequence	• What caused the event to happen? • What was the result or consequence of the event? • Who was affected by it?
Continuity and Change	• What changed over time? • What stayed the same, or did not change?
Patterns and Trends	• What characteristics do I notice that are similar and repeat? • What connections can I make among these patterns? • What trends do I notice happening over time?
Interrelationships	• What connections do I see? • What positive and negative effects do I notice within these connections?
Perspective	• What perspectives do I see? • Whose perspectives are these? • What is my perspective?

You can use more than one thinking concept at a time. For example, when you think about an event's significance, you may also identify different perspectives on the event.

Catholic Social Teachings

These Catholic social teachings should guide your thinking about social studies.

When You Think about the Catholic Social Teaching of ...	You Might Ask Yourself ...
The Dignity of the Human Person	• How do people care for and respect one another? • How does this show that they are honouring God?
The Person as Part of a Family and a Community	• What goals do people share? • How do they work together?
The Person's Role in the Common Good	• What do people do to help one another?
The Person's Rights and Responsibilities	• What rights do people have? • What responsibilities do people have?
The Person's Special Responsibility to the Poor and Vulnerable	• How do people care for one another, especially those in need or suffering?
The Person as God's Manager, Worker, and Steward of Creation	• How do people act as stewards of Creation? • How do they respect the gifts that God gives us?

Exploring *Many Gifts* 3

Here are some of the features you will see in this book.

The **Unit Opener** introduces the unit.

The **Big Question** is what you will be thinking about throughout the unit.

The **Our Faith** quotation shows the Catholic perspective for the unit.

Let's Talk pages introduce the unit and chapters. They help you think about what you already know and make predictions.

In **Father Mike Says …**, the Catholic social teaching for the unit is explained.

Looking Ahead to the Unit Inquiry tells you about the Unit Inquiry activity at the end of the unit.

The **chapter inquiry question** is the guiding question for the chapter.

The **learning goals** tell you what you will learn in the chapter.

Headings introduce new topics.

Learn about the **social studies thinking concepts**.

Sticky notes help you apply your learning about the social studies thinking concepts.

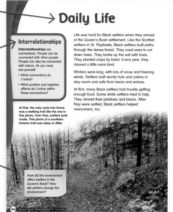

Inquiry pages focus on the inquiry process and other skills.

At the end of each chapter, you think about and show your learning in **Pulling It Together**.

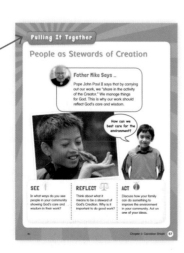

Each **Catholic Connection** links the social studies topics to our Catholic faith.

Each section ends with one **I Wonder ...** or **Try It** question for reflection and discussion.

Each **Faith in Action** gives an example of Ontario Catholic students living their faith.

New **vocabulary words** appear in bold and in the Glossary.

In the **Unit Inquiry**, you investigate a topic that interests you.

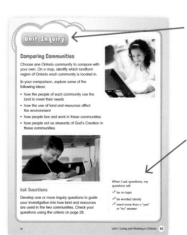

Checklists remind you what to do during each part of the process.

Living and Working in Ontario

Ontario is made up of three landform regions. Each region has features that make it different from the other regions. People care for God's Creation as they live and work in communities across the province.

Our Faith

Saint John Paul II said ...

When people work, they not only change things and society, they also develop themselves.

On Human Work, no. 26

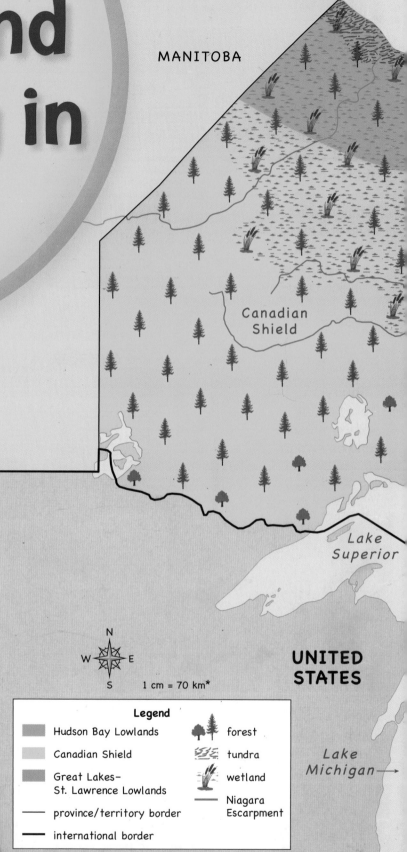

MANITOBA

Canadian Shield

Lake Superior

UNITED STATES

Lake Michigan →

N
W   E
S

1 cm = 70 km*

Legend

▓	Hudson Bay Lowlands	🌲	forest
▓	Canadian Shield	≈	tundra
▓	Great Lakes–St. Lawrence Lowlands	⚘	wetland
──	province/territory border	—	Niagara Escarpment
━━	international border		

* Each cm on this map represents 70 km on the ground.

Landform Regions of Ontario

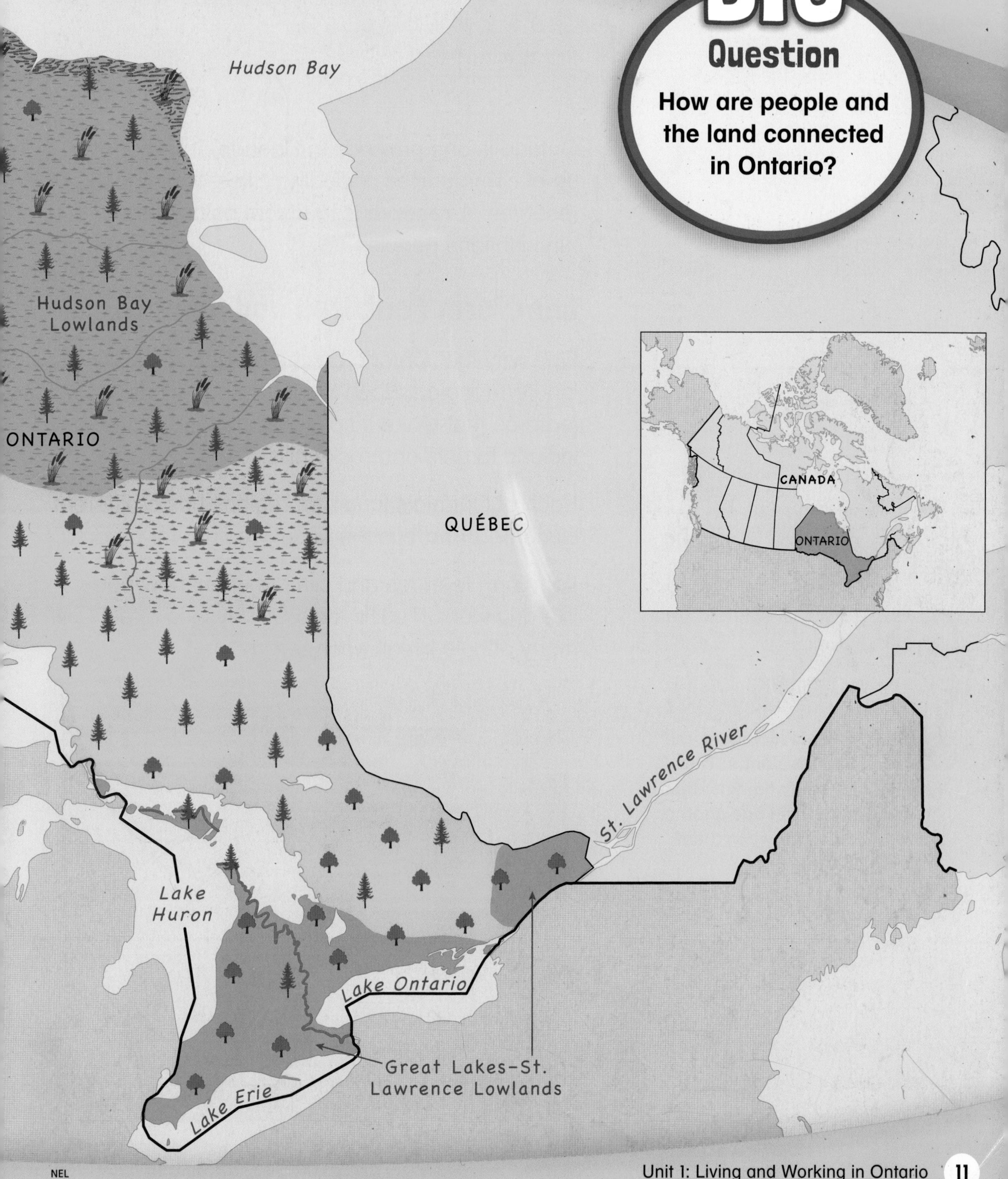

Hudson Bay

Hudson Bay Lowlands

ONTARIO

QUÉBEC

CANADA

ONTARIO

St. Lawrence River

Lake Huron

Lake Ontario

Great Lakes–St. Lawrence Lowlands

Lake Erie

BIG
Question

How are people and the land connected in Ontario?

Three Landform Regions

Ontario is one province in Canada. It is made up of communities, including cities, towns, and reserves. A **reserve** is land that belongs to First Nations peoples.

Landform Features and Climate

One way that Ontario can be divided is by landform region. Each landform region has features that make it special. Landform features include forests and rocky hills.

Each of Ontario's landform regions has a different climate. **Climate** is the usual weather for an area.

Landform features and climate affect how people live and work in each region. They also affect how many people live in each region.

Attawapiskat is located in the Hudson Bay Lowlands. This region has small communities. Many are far from one another, and travelling between them can be difficult.

Land Use

In each landform region, people use land in similar ways. For example, in each region, land is used for housing, parks, schools, and roads.

There are also differences in how land is used. For example, most farms in Ontario are found in the Great Lakes–St. Lawrence Lowlands. The soil there is good for growing and the climate is warmer than the other regions.

How land is used affects how people live and work in a community. The more we understand how we use land in our communities, the better we can act as stewards of God's Creation.

Sault Ste. Marie is located in the Canadian Shield. This region has small and large communities and some cities. It is Ontario's largest landform region.

Mississauga is located in the Great Lakes–St. Lawrence Lowlands. This region has small and large communities with many large cities. This region has the highest population in Ontario.

Life in Ontario

Make connections between these activities and the landform regions.

Hudson Bay Lowlands

Canadian Shield

Great Lakes–St. Lawrence Lowlands

Unit 1: Living and Working in Ontario

Father Mike Says...

God created Earth. We create a home for people by our work. We are stewards of God's Creation. In this unit, you will look at how we act as stewards in different parts of Ontario.

Looking Ahead to the Unit Inquiry

At the end of this unit, you will be asked to complete an investigation of two Ontario communities. You will compare the community where you live now with another community in Ontario. In your comparison, you will explore some of the following ideas:

- how the two communities use the land and resources
- how the use of land and resources affects the environment
- how the land helps people meet their needs
- how people live and work in these communities
- how people act as stewards of God's Creation to protect the environment

At the end of the investigation, you will share your findings.

Hudson Bay Lowlands

Our Faith

The Bible says ...

" The Earth is the Lord's and all that is in it, the world, and those who live in it. "

Psalm 24:1 (NRSV)

Hi, my name is Sarah. I wonder: How do we care for God's Creation?

In this chapter, you will

- describe how people in this region use the land to meet their needs

- ask questions

- analyze and construct maps

- make connections between features of the land and how they are used

- reflect on how people are stewards of Creation

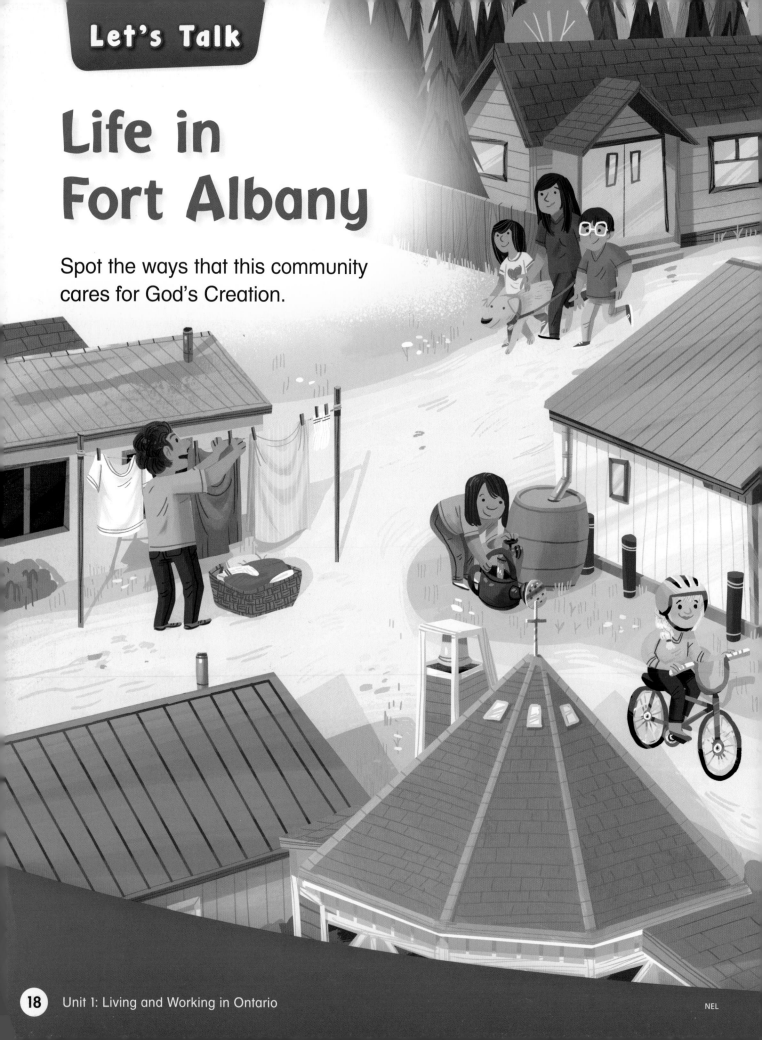

Life in Fort Albany

Spot the ways that this community cares for God's Creation.

Features of the Region

Landform Features

The land in the Hudson Bay Lowlands is flat and lower than the land in other regions nearby. Most of the land is covered in wetlands or tundra. **Wetlands** are watery swamps and marshes. **Tundra** is flat land with no trees. In tundra, the ground stays frozen for most of the year.

Climate

Winters in the Hudson Bay Lowlands are very cold. Ice covers much of this region. Summers are warm, but not hot.

Catholic Connection

The Bible tells us that God wants us to be responsible in caring for, and using, the environment. God also wants the environment to be home to all of his Creation.

The wetlands in this region have a lot of moss and other plants that grow in and on top of the water.

It is hard for trees to grow in tundra because the ground is frozen for most of the year. This photo shows trees growing past the edge of the tundra.

Landform Features of Ontario's Hudson Bay Lowlands

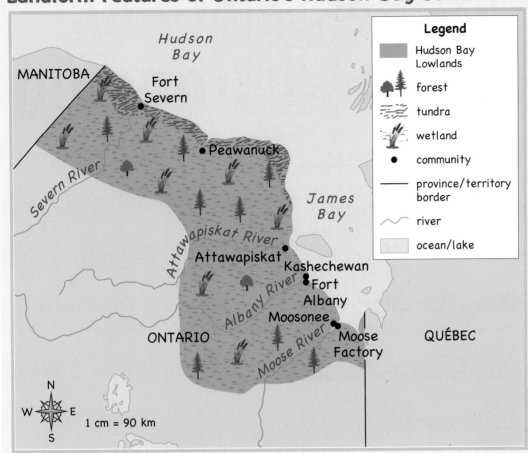

Legend

	Hudson Bay Lowlands
	forest
	tundra
	wetland
●	community
—	province/territory border
	river
	ocean/lake

Hudson Bay

MANITOBA

Fort Severn

Peawanuck

Severn River

Attawapiskat River

Attawapiskat

James Bay

Kashechewan

Fort Albany

Albany River

Moosonee

ONTARIO

Moose River

Moose Factory

QUÉBEC

N W E S

1 cm = 90 km

Natural Resources

Natural resources are things found in nature that are valuable or useful to people. These resources are part of God's Creation and must be used wisely.

Water, animals, and minerals are some of the natural resources found in this region. **Minerals** are materials found in the ground. Some minerals in this region are diamonds and iron.

Caribou and many other animals live in the Hudson Bay Lowlands.

I Wonder...

How do people use natural resources to meet their needs?

Land Use: Fishing, Hunting, and Trapping

Many First Nations peoples live in the Hudson Bay Lowlands. They have lived there for thousands of years. Many people work to fish, hunt, and trap animals in this region. To **trap** means to catch animals.

Effects of Fishing, Hunting, and Trapping

Animals provide food for families who live in the Hudson Bay Lowlands. Animal fur and skin are used for clothing. The clothing helps people keep warm during the cold winter. Some people sell what they catch.

These hunters look for bears at a camp near Peawanuck.

People in the region also work as guides. They help tourists fish, hunt, and trap.

First Nations peoples believe that it is important to care for the environment. They teach others how to respect the land and natural resources.

Most fishers, hunters, and trappers limit the number of animals they catch. If too many animals are caught, there will be less for people to share. This would affect the people who depend on those animals to live. It could also affect other animals living in the area.

Faith in Action

Each spring, at Sacred Heart Catholic School in Kirkland Lake, Ontario, students live their faith by caring for God's Creation. They clean up garbage around the school and plant flowers in the garden. Their actions care for the land and allow all students to enjoy nature in their community.

People fish all year long in the region. In winter, they cut holes in the ice to reach the fish below.

I Wonder ...

Why is it important to take care of the land?

Chapter 1: Hudson Bay Lowlands **23**

Land Use: Transportation

Significance

When something is **significant**, it is important. People, things, events, and places can all be significant. What is significant for one group may not be significant for another. For example, you may think that your nearby park is significant because you often play there. Someone living in another community may not think that it is significant. As you read, ask yourself

• What is significant?

• Who is it significant to?

• Why is it significant?

Transportation means ways that people and things are moved from one place to another. In this region, swampy wetlands and frozen tundra make it impossible to build dirt roads to connect most communities. Instead, ice roads are built on frozen land and water. Ice roads can only be used at certain times of the year.

Planes bring people and goods into this region all year long. **Goods** are items that are made for people to use. In warmer weather, some people use boats to get around. Cars can travel on roads within communities. Only Moosonee is connected to other regions by a railroad.

Planes and ice roads are significant to this region.

This truck uses an ice road to travel between Moosonee and Moose Factory. Trucks use ice roads to deliver food and fuel to communities.

Effects of Transportation

Transportation connects people to others in their community. It connects them to other communities.

Some people in this region work in transportation. They work as delivery drivers and boat taxi drivers, and at airports.

How people travel affects the environment. Boats, trucks, and planes use a lot of fuel. This creates pollution. Limiting travel can help to reduce air and water pollution.

Fuel is significant to everyone who lives in this region. Why do you think it is significant?

Transportation in Ontario's Hudson Bay Lowlands

MANITOBA

Hudson Bay

Fort Severn

Peawanuck

Severn River

Legend

Hudson Bay Lowlands

✈ airport

～ ice road

railroad

● community

Attawapiskat River

James Bay

Attawapiskat

Kashechewan

Fort Albany

QUÉBEC

Albany River

ONTARIO

Moosonee
Moose Factory

Moose River

N
W E
S

1 cm = 90 km

I Wonder...

How is transportation significant to different people in this region?

Welcome to

Attawapiskat

Population: 1549

Attawapiskat

Attawapiskat is a small community on the Attawapiskat First Nation reserve. Forests and wetlands surround Attawapiskat. Finding work here can be hard. Some people work in education or at the nearby diamond mine.

Land Use: Recreation

One way that the land is used in Attawapiskat is for recreation. Using land for **recreation** means that it is used for play and enjoyable activities. Attawapiskat has a sports field, an arena, a community hall, and a gym. There are also open spaces for hiking and skiing.

Children play baseball in Attawapiskat.

Communities

Moosonee

The small town of Moosonee is located on the Moose River. Forests and wetlands surround Moosonee. Some people in Moosonee work in schools, at the hospital, and for the local government. Other people work at hotels, restaurants, and tourist sites.

Land Use: Recreation

Moosonee has soccer and baseball fields and a recreation centre. An arena and curling rink are open in fall and winter. There are open spaces for skiing and hiking. In summer, boats are docked along the waterfront for boat tours.

Tourists visiting Moosonee can look for beluga whales in the Moose River.

Welcome to

Moosonee

Population: 1725

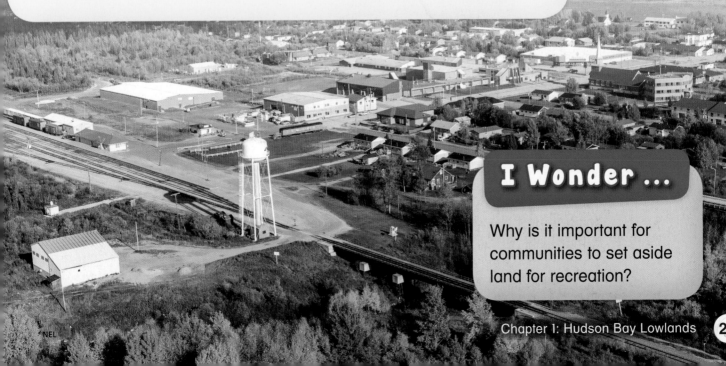

I Wonder ...

Why is it important for communities to set aside land for recreation?

Ask Questions

Asking questions helps you find answers to things you wonder about. You might have a lot of questions about a topic. So, how do you know what a good inquiry question is?

I wonder what happens when land is used for recreation.

Steps for Asking Inquiry Questions

1 Think about the topic. What do you already know? What do you want to learn?

2 Think of possible questions. Write them down.

3 Check each of the questions using criteria such as the following:

- A good question is on topic.
- A good question is worded clearly.
- A good question must be answered with more than a "yes" or "no."

Sarah Investigates

Sarah wondered about the effects of using land for recreation in the Hudson Bay Lowlands. She thought of what she already knew about recreation in the region. Then, she started a list of questions that she might use for her investigation.

My Questions
What different kinds of transportation are in the Hudson Bay Lowlands?
Do all the communities have pools?
Are there any hockey teams in this region?
How is the land hurt by people?
What are good and bad effects of using the land for recreation?

Sarah wondered which question she should use for her inquiry. She used the inquiry question criteria in step 3 to help her decide.

As Sarah investigates her topic, she may have new questions. She may decide to change her inquiry question because of what she learns.

Try It

1. Use the criteria in step 3 to judge Sarah's questions.

2. Which of Sarah's questions works best? Explain why you think it is the best question.

Working in the Hudson Bay Lowlands

Perspective

Perspective is how people see things. It is their point of view. People's perspectives depend on their beliefs and experiences. As you read, ask yourself

- What perspectives do I see?
- Whose perspectives are these?
- What is my perspective?

Lianne
Nurse
Moosonee

I work as a community nurse. In my work, I help people who need healthcare in their homes. I connect patients with other healthcare and support workers. I care for all my patients in their homes so they do not have to visit a doctor's office or hospital. I enjoy teaching people about their health and safety.

David
Business Development Coordinator
Fort Albany

I work for the band council of the Fort Albany First Nation. A **band council** is a group of people who make decisions on how the land is used on a reserve. I help businesses that would like to come to Fort Albany. I also help the businesses already in the community. I love the challenge of finding solutions that help both businesses and the people of our community.

Whose perspectives does David consider in his work?

Donna
Regional Council Executive Director
Moose Factory

A **regional council** is a group of people who make decisions for a region. The Mushkegowuk Council is made up of people from the eight First Nations of the Hudson Bay Lowlands. Our council looks after needs, such as education, work, and land use. I am responsible for a staff of 50 people. The best part of my job is working with the caring people on the council.

Jeff
Hunter
Moose Factory

I learned how to hunt and gather from my grandparents. I use traditional knowledge from my people, the Moose Cree. I love being able to live according to the old ways. I love being out on the land. Also, I love teaching my kids and kids in the community these traditional ways.

What is Jeff's perspective on traditions?

I Wonder...

As a Catholic, what connections can I make to these perspectives?

Inquiry

Analyze and Construct Maps

Maps usually show how an area looks from above. They can show how land is used and where things are. Maps have features that help you understand the information.

A **title** describes the information on the map.

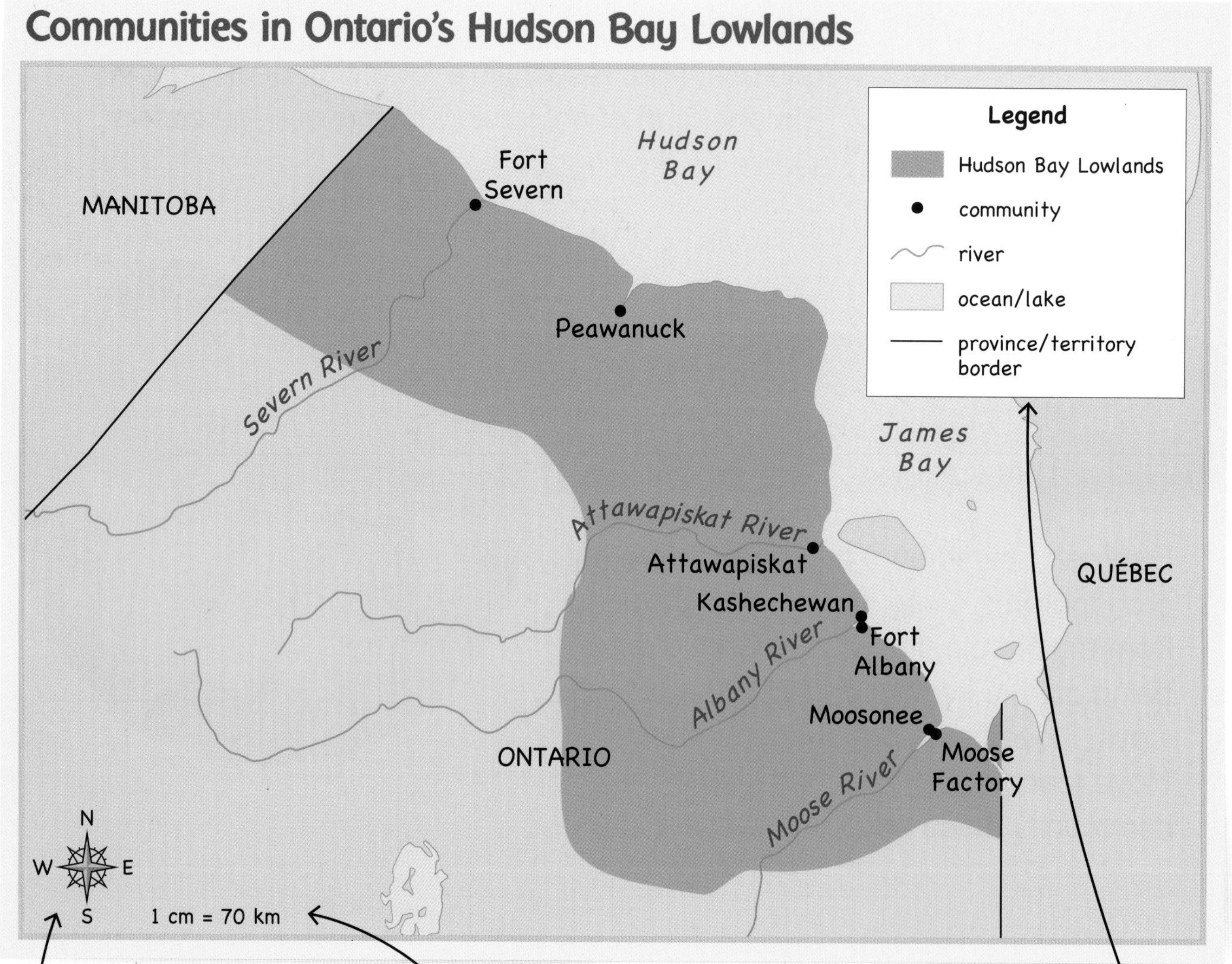

Communities in Ontario's Hudson Bay Lowlands

Hudson Bay

MANITOBA

Fort Severn

Severn River

Peawanuck

Legend

Hudson Bay Lowlands

• community

river

ocean/lake

province/territory border

James Bay

QUÉBEC

Attawapiskat River

Attawapiskat

Kashechewan

Albany River

Fort Albany

Moosonee

Moose Factory

ONTARIO

Moose River

N
W E
S

1 cm = 70 km

A **compass rose** shows which way is north, south, east, and west.

A **scale** represents distance.

A **legend** explains symbols, colours, lines, and labels.

Sarah Investigates

Sarah used an outline map from her teacher to create a map of her community. She lives in Moose Factory, which is on an island. She did research to find out what to include on her map.

I want to create a map to show how land is used in my community.

Land Use in Moose Factory

Moose River

Moose River

1 cm = 700 m

Legend
- forest
- recreation
- housing
- commerce
- church
- tourism
- healthcare
- school
- other
- • helicopter pad

Sarah noticed that more land is used for housing than for commerce.

Try It

1. Create a map of your schoolyard. Make sure that you include map features such as a title, legend, scale, and compass rose.

2. Use your map to help you figure out the best spot for a wildlife habitat garden.

Challenges and Opportunities

Which of these photos do you think reflect the challenges of living and working in this region? Which photos reflect the opportunities? Which photos show both?

work

transportation

environment

communication

I Wonder ...

How do people living in this region meet their needs?

People as Stewards of Creation

Father Mike Says ...

God created us in His image so that, as part of His family, we could care for His world. Each of us has our own special gifts to help make this a better world.

> How can I act as God's steward in my community?

SEE

Many people in the Hudson Bay Lowlands act to protect the land. Where do you see people in your community acting as good stewards?

REFLECT

Why is it important to act as a good steward?

ACT

Think of one way you can protect the land where you live. Act on it.

What I Discovered

Draw a picture to show what you have learned about the Hudson Bay Lowlands. Include labels.

Making Connections

What different land uses do you notice in your community? Which land use do you think is most significant?

Chapter Inquiry

① Choose one section from the chapter to review. Examine any images or maps.

② Write down three questions you have after reviewing the section. Try to ask questions that help you think deeply about the land and how people act as God's stewards.

③ Use the criteria on page 28 to decide which of your questions is best to start an investigation. If none of your questions match the criteria, think of a question that does.

This photo shows homes on a typical street in Fort Albany.

Canadian Shield

Our Faith

The Bible says ...

"Let the Earth bless the Lord, let it sing praise to him and highly exalt him forever."

Daniel 3:74 (NRSV)

Hi, my name is Dominic. I wonder: How do people's activities affect God's Creation?

In this chapter, you will

- identify major types of work in this region
- gather and organize information
- interpret and analyze information
- describe some connections between the land in this region and types of communities
- reflect on how people are stewards of Creation

Effects on God's Creation

Make connections between these photos of the Canadian Shield.

Features of the Region

Landform Features

The Canadian Shield is the largest landform region in Ontario. It is mostly covered by rock. There are many hills. Some parts of this region do not have much soil. Only a few parts are good for farming. This region has many lakes, rivers, forests, and wetlands.

In Ontario, there are more people living in the Canadian Shield than in the Hudson Bay Lowlands.

Landform Features of Ontario's Canadian Shield

Legend

- Canadian Shield
- forest
- wetland
- community
- ocean/lake
- river
- international border
- province/territory border

MANITOBA

Pickle Lake

Red Lake

Kenora

Lake of the Woods

Lake Nipigon

ONTARIO

Terrace Bay

Thunder Bay

Marathon

Timmins

Lake Superior

UNITED STATES

Lake Michigan

Espanola

Sudbury

Lake Huron

Whitefish Lake First Nation

Lake Nipissing

QUÉBEC

Parry Sound

Gravenhurst

Buckhorn

N W E S

1 cm = 100 km

Climate

This region has cold winters. In the north part of this region, summers are warm. In the south part, summers are hot.

Natural Resources

In this region, the gifts of God include trees, water, and minerals. Trees are used for paper and wood products. Gold and nickel are two of the minerals found in the Canadian Shield. Minerals are used to make things like coins and jewellery. Resources from the area are used in local communities and around the world.

Black bears live in this region. Wolves, beavers, woodland caribou, and many other types of animals also live there.

Many people visit the Canadian Shield to swim, fish, and hike. This lake is on the Whitefish Lake First Nation. How can tourists visit the region and take care of it at the same time?

Faith in Action

Students participated in a project to protect the wetlands behind St. Joseph's Catholic School in Clinton, Ontario. They planted trees around the wetlands to shield the area from wind. Since 2011, over 3000 trees have been planted by students and other volunteers.

I Wonder...

How does this region compare with the Hudson Bay Lowlands?

Land Use: Forestry

Forestry means planting, managing, and using trees. People cut down and use trees in the forests of the Canadian Shield to make wood and paper products.

From Tree to Chair to Tree

Forest managers take care of the land. They think about the environment and the number of trees that should be cut down.

Loggers cut down the trees. The trees are transported to other parts of the region or province.

Sawmill workers cut the trees into smaller pieces. The pieces are used to make wood products.

Furniture makers use the wood from the trees to make things like chairs.

Tree planters plant young, small trees in areas where trees have been cut down.

Effects of Forestry

Many people work in forestry in the Canadian Shield. Trees provide people with many useful wood and paper products. Some examples are books, furniture, and musical instruments.

Some people in the Canadian Shield work in paper mills. This paper mill in Espanola makes over 200 different types of paper.

Cutting down too many trees may damage an area. Animals in the area may lose their homes. Plants that grow near the trees may be affected, too. Sometimes, pollution from paper mills and sawmills goes into the air and water.

People can try to reduce the number of trees being cut down. They can reuse and recycle paper and wood products. These actions can help to stop some items from becoming garbage. These actions can also reduce pollution.

Catholic Connection

The Bible teaches us that Creation is a gift from God. We need to care for it so that everyone may enjoy it equally. If we use too many of the trees in the Canadian Shield, then there will not be enough left for people in the future.

I Wonder ...

What products that come from forests do I use?

Land Use: Mining

Cause and Consequence

A **cause** is something that makes an event happen. A **consequence** happens as a result of that event. For example, cutting down trees in an area results in animals losing their homes.

As you read, ask yourself

- What caused the event to happen?
- What was the result or consequence of the event?
- Who was affected by it?

What could be some of the consequences of mining in a new area?

The land in this region is full of minerals, such as gold, copper, iron, and nickel. Some of the land is used for mining. **Mining** is the removal of minerals from the ground.

Effects of Mining

Mining creates work in the Canadian Shield. Scientists study rocks to find the minerals. Before a new mine is created, experts think about how it will affect the environment. They make plans to reduce any negative effects. Later, workers are needed to build and run the mine. Pickle Lake is one example of a community that was built because gold and copper mines opened nearby.

This gold mine is located near the town of Marathon. As the broken rock is dug up, the minerals are taken out.

Many of the things we use every day are made with minerals. For example, minerals are used to make items such as car parts, wires for electricity, and sunscreen.

After minerals are taken out of the ground, they cannot be replaced. When there are no minerals left, mines close. Some closed mines leave big holes in the land. Thousands of people lose their jobs. Many people must leave to find work in other communities.

Mining also creates pollution that goes into the air, water, and ground. Pollution affects the plants, animals, and people in the area. Mining companies and communities try to work together to solve these problems.

When the minerals are gone from an area, mines close. Who might be affected by this consequence?

Many communities, such as the city of Timmins, depend on mining for work. This photo shows a gold mine near Timmins.

I Wonder...

How can we use minerals and still protect God's Creation?

Chapter 2: Canadian Shield   **45**

Gather and Organize Information

What are some of the consequences when people visit parks in this region?

Steps for Gathering Information

1. Think about the information you need.

2. Identify sources you can use, for example, books, magazines, websites, maps, photos, and videos.

3. Choose sources you can trust, such as a community website.

Dominic Investigates

Dominic thought about where to look for information about the effects of visitors on parks. He checked different sources, such as the website for the Georgian Bay Islands National Park. He found out that about 40 000 people visit the park each year. He also found out that campers pay fees to stay at the park. These fees help pay for staff to care for the park.

Dominic found this information about bears on the park website.

YOU ARE IN **BLACK BEAR** COUNTRY

Keep the "Wild" in Wildlife

Do not disturb wildlife. Give animals space.

Do not feed wildlife. It is illegal to feed wildlife in a national park. Wild animals find healthy food in their natural environment.

Keep your campsite clean. Do not leave food out. Store garbage in a vehicle or the park's bear-proof garbage containers.

Steps for Organizing Information

1 Organize the information to help you understand it. Sort your information into categories by putting similar ideas together. Sometimes, it helps to use an organizer.

2 Check that you have enough information.

Dominic Investigates

Dominic thought about different ways he could sort the information into categories. He decided to organize the information into positive and negative effects of park visitors.

Positive Effects of Visitors	Negative Effects of Visitors
• Visitors help to create work for people in the community. • A large number of people get to experience nature.	• A large number of visitors can create more pollution. • Garbage left by visitors can attract and hurt wildlife.

Try It

1 What questions do you have about forestry and mining? Gather information about foresty and mining from pages 42 to 45.

2 Organize the information to make it easier to understand.

Working in the Canadian Shield

Spencer
Miner
Sudbury

I work in nickel and copper mines. The work can be dangerous. It gets very hot underground, but I love working there. I love the challenge of drilling and blasting rocks. I enjoy seeing the results of my work. When an area of rock has been removed and I get the minerals out, I feel great.

Curniss
Environmental Researcher
Thunder Bay

I am an environmental researcher for the city of Thunder Bay. I investigate how people's activities affect the land. I look for ways to make Thunder Bay more "green," or more environmentally friendly. I believe it is important to think about the environment when you are planning events or city projects. I love doing something I care so much about.

Donna
Health Promoter
Kenora

I am a health promoter for a First Nations health access centre. I teach and promote health and wellness. I believe that everyone should know about the importance of handwashing, eating well, and staying active.

Dave
Fishing Lodge Manager
Red Lake

I manage a fishing lodge. I make sure the lodge runs smoothly for our guests. Part of my work is telling guests the rules of the lodge. For example, on some lakes, fishers cannot keep the fish they catch. Instead, they must release the fish back into the lake. This is to make sure there are always fish.

I Wonder ...

What type of work in the Canadian Shield would I want to do?

Welcome to

Sudbury

**Population:
160 770**

Sudbury

Sudbury is a big city surrounded by lakes and forests. Many people work in mining. Other people work in healthcare, education, banking, and tourism.

Land Use: Commerce

Some of the land in Sudbury is used for commerce. **Commerce** means buying and selling things for money. When land is used for commerce, it is used for stores, restaurants, and other businesses. In Sudbury, there are many areas with businesses.

Downtown Sudbury has a mix of homes and businesses that are close together.

Communities

Terrace Bay

Terrace Bay is a small community surrounded by forests. Many people work at the mill, where wood is turned into paper. Other people work in construction or other businesses, such as restaurants. Visitors come in the summer to enjoy the beaches, hiking trails, and golf course.

Land Use: Commerce

Most of the businesses in Terrace Bay are grouped together in a small area on the town's main street. The street is just off the highway. This makes it easy for people driving by Terrace Bay to find the town's stores, gas stations, restaurants, and banks.

Welcome to

Terrace Bay

Population: 1466

Many of the stores in Terrace Bay are located in this plaza.

I Wonder...

How do people decide what stores to open in a community?

Interpret and Analyze Information

When you interpret, you think about what the information means. When you analyze, you dig deeper into a topic to understand it better.

Steps for Interpreting and Analyzing Information

1 Put the information into your own words.

2 Think about the meaning of the information. Look for patterns and connections to help you understand the meaning.

3 State your new understanding.

Why are snapping turtles in this region at risk?

Dominic Investigates

Dominic found out that snapping turtles are at risk in the Canadian Shield. When an animal is at risk, it is in danger of becoming extinct. He wanted to know more. Dominic found some information on a website.

Turtles in Danger

Pollution created by people and businesses harms snapping turtles. When new homes and roads are built on wetlands, turtles can lose their homes. When turtles cross roads to find a mate or lay eggs, they can get hit.

Dominic put the information into his own words.

Snapping turtles are a species at risk because of three things:

- People create pollution.

- Turtles' homes are disappearing because of construction.

- People drive cars and trucks that kill turtles on roads.

This turtle is using an ecopassage in Long Point. An *ecopassage* is a bridge or tunnel over or under a highway, which has been built to protect wildlife. This tunnel under a road helps turtles and snakes safely cross the road.

Dominic thought about the information he found. He looked for patterns and connections in the information. After he analyzed his list, Dominic's new understanding was that all the reasons were connected to people's activities.

Try It

1. Look at the information about Sudbury and Terrace Bay on pages 50 and 51.

2. Compare the communities. Use the steps for interpreting and analyzing.

3. State your new understanding.

Land Use: Recreation

People who live in the Canadian Shield also use land for recreation. Many visitors come to this region, especially in summer.

Tour boats, like this one in Gravenhurst, take visitors to see the beauty and wildlife of the region.

In this photo, students participate in a race in Timmins. Events and games are held on trails and fields built by communities.

Camping in provincial parks is a popular activity in the Canadian Shield. In this photo, a family is canoeing in Killbear Provincial Park.

Effects of Recreation

Recreation creates work for people in the Canadian Shield. When people visit communities for recreation, they need places to stay and places to eat. People living there also enjoy the many parks and open spaces.

When people visit parks and other natural areas, they may harm the land. Leaving garbage and picking plants can hurt the animals and plants that live there.

In this photo, people enjoy a sleigh ride at a festival in Buckhorn. Festivals and carnivals bring people of all cultures together to enjoy activities.

Many communities provide playgrounds for children to enjoy. This playground is in Parry Sound. Community workers make sure playgrounds are kept clean and safe.

I Wonder...

How is land used for recreation in my community?

On the Water

Many communities in the Canadian Shield are on the shores of rivers or lakes. Their waterfronts are used for different purposes.

- Some communities, like Sudbury, have businesses and homes on their waterfronts.
- Some communities, like Elliot Lake, have beaches for recreation.
- Some communities, like Thunder Bay, use their waterfronts for shipping goods and transportation.

How communities use waterfronts can affect the water in rivers and lakes. Garbage and gas from boats can cause water pollution.

Most of Kenora's waterfront is used for recreation, with parks, marinas, and walking trails. Tourists visit to enjoy fishing, boat cruises, and sandy beaches.

Large ships travel from Thunder Bay through the Great Lakes and out to the Atlantic Ocean. They carry goods, such as coal, grains, and forest products.

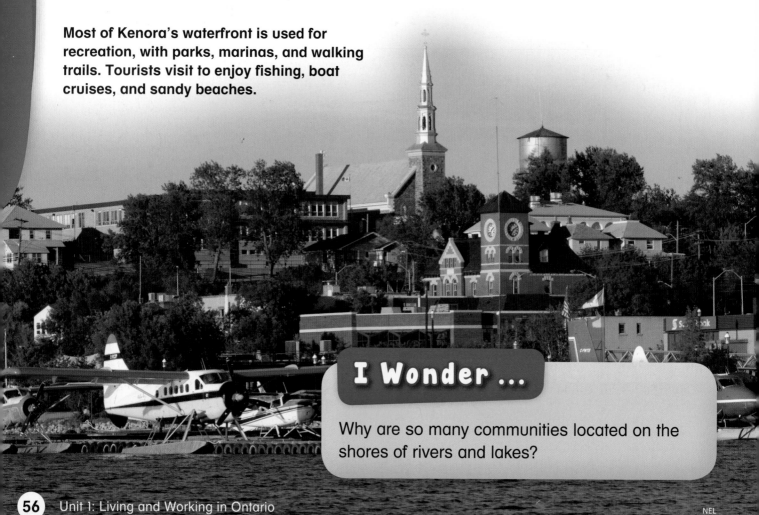

I Wonder ...

Why are so many communities located on the shores of rivers and lakes?

People as Stewards of Creation

Father Mike Says ...

Pope John Paul II says that by carrying out our work, we "share in the activity of the Creator." We manage things for God. This is why our work should reflect God's care and wisdom.

How can we best care for the environment?

SEE

In what ways do you see people in your community showing God's care and wisdom in their work?

REFLECT

Think about what it means to be a steward of God's Creation. Why is it important to do good work?

ACT

Discuss how your family can do something to improve the environment in your community. Act on one of your ideas.

What I Discovered

Use a graphic organizer to show how people's activities affect God's Creation in the Canadian Shield. Some examples of graphic organizers are shown here.

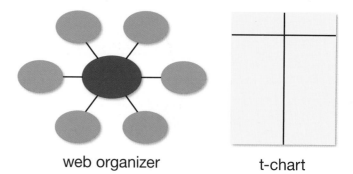

web organizer

t-chart

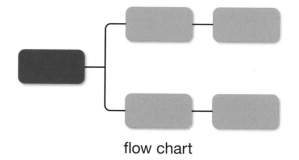

flow chart

 ## Making Connections

Think about the natural resources in the Canadian Shield. How do you use these resources in your daily life?

 ## Chapter Inquiry

1. Review the questions you developed in the Chapter Inquiry for Chapter 1. What new questions do you have?

2. Gather information from Chapter 2 to answer one of your questions. Organize the information.

3. Interpret and analyze the information you find.

Chapter 3

Great Lakes–St. Lawrence Lowlands

Our Faith

❝We must do our best to work hard, to be fair and honest, and to look after those in need.❞

Catechism of the Catholic Church 2239

Hi, my name is Ella. I wonder: Why do people live and work where they do?

In this chapter, you will

- identify how communities in this region use land to meet people's needs and wants

- analyze maps

- evaluate and draw conclusions

- explore relationships between work and natural resources in this region

- reflect on how people work for the common good

Products of Work

Look at the photos. Match the workers
to the products.

Features of the Region

Landform Features

The Great Lakes–St. Lawrence Lowlands is the smallest landform region in Ontario. This region is located in the southern part of the province. Most of the land in this region is low and flat. Some parts, such as the Niagara Escarpment, have hills and cliffs. The rich soil makes this region ideal for farming.

The Niagara Escarpment is a long, rocky area made up of tall cliffs.

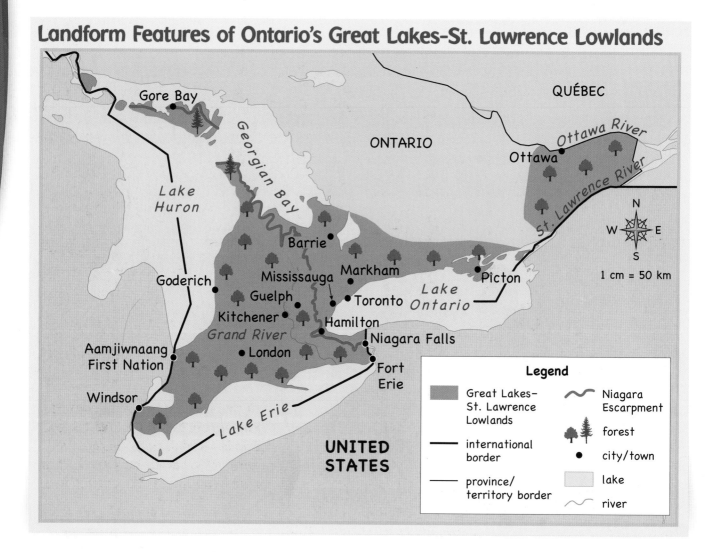

Landform Features of Ontario's Great Lakes-St. Lawrence Lowlands

Gore Bay

QUÉBEC

Lake Huron

Georgian Bay

ONTARIO

Ottawa River

Ottawa

St. Lawrence River

N
W   E
S

1 cm = 50 km

Barrie

Goderich

Mississauga   Markham

Picton

Lake Ontario

Guelph   Toronto

Kitchener

Hamilton

Grand River

Niagara Falls

Aamjiwnaang First Nation

London

Fort Erie

Windsor

Lake Erie

UNITED STATES

Legend

- ▨ Great Lakes–St. Lawrence Lowlands
- ～ Niagara Escarpment
- 🌲 forest
- —— international border
- ● city/town
- ▨ lake
- —— province/territory border
- ～ river

Climate

In this region, temperatures are warm in spring and fall, and hot in summer. There is a lot of rain in spring. Winter is cold and snowy. In this region, it does not get as cold as it does in the Canadian Shield and Hudson Bay Lowlands.

Natural Resources

There are many gifts from God in this region, including water. The region is named after the huge lakes called the Great Lakes and the wide St. Lawrence River. Water provides transportation routes and electricity.

Many animals live in this region, such as foxes, coyotes, and hawks. This region also has minerals, such as salt.

Construction in communities can cause animals to lose their homes. However, some animals, such as the beaver, are able to adapt. This beaver was seen in the city of Guelph.

I Wonder ...

What is special about this region that makes people want to live there?

At this mine in Goderich, salt is taken from beneath Lake Huron. Salt is used to help keep winter roads clear of ice and snow. It is also used to add flavour to food.

Living and Working in the Region

Patterns and Trends

Patterns are characteristics that are similar and repeat. Patterns can be found in nature or created by humans. One pattern you may notice is that many communities are located near water.

Trends are patterns that happen over a period of time. One trend you may notice is that each year, more houses are being built in your community. As you read, ask yourself

- What characteristics do I notice that are similar and repeat?
- What connections can I make among these patterns?
- What trends do I notice happening over time?

Many communities in this region are located along the St. Lawrence River and near the Great Lakes. Being near water makes it easy to grow food and ship goods by boat.

Today, the Great Lakes–St. Lawrence Lowlands has the highest population of any region in Canada. There are many large cities in this region, such as Toronto, Mississauga, and Ottawa. Many different types of housing, transportation, and work are available.

Some people work in banks, hospitals, and universities. Businesses that develop technology are also based in this region.

Mississauga has many tall towers used for homes and offices.

How People Affect the Land

People move to bigger cities and towns for many reasons. Larger populations affect the land and how it is used. Cities and towns must plan ahead. They need to balance their communities' needs and wants and still protect God's Creation.

Having more people in an area means more food, more homes, and more water are needed. Homes, roads, and stores are sometimes built on land that was used for farming.

Larger populations also create more garbage and pollution. This affects wetlands, forests, and the plants and animals that live there.

When more people move to a city or town every year, the population grows. This is a trend.

When more homes are built, more garbage and pollution are created. This is a pattern.

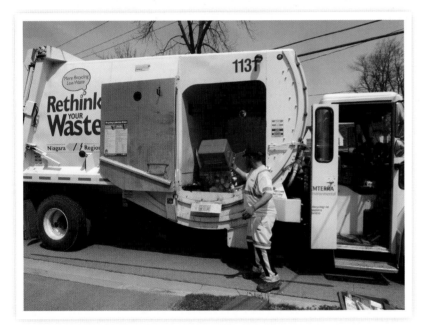

Most communities in Ontario reduce some of their garbage by collecting materials for recycling. This worker collects materials for recycling in Fort Erie.

Faith in Action

Each year, the Niagara Catholic District School Board in Ontario hosts a recycling event. Students can show their care for God's Creation by recycling unwanted electronic devices. All funds raised by this event go to help families in need.

I Wonder...

What patterns do I notice in my community?

Analyze Maps

Maps can show where things are located in relation to each other. When you analyze a map, you look at its parts and try to make sense of it.

Steps for Analyzing Maps

1. Read the title of the map. The title tells you the map's purpose.
2. Look at the features of the map, including the legend. The legend shows what the symbols and colours mean.
3. Compare different parts of the map. Look for patterns. Make connections.
4. Identify what you learned from the map.

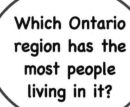

Which Ontario region has the most people living in it?

Ella Investigates

Ella wanted to understand what this population map of Ontario is showing. She read the title. The legend told her that one dot represents 1000 people.

Then, Ella compared different parts of the map and noticed a pattern. Some parts had so many dots that they blended together. From the map, she learned that most people live in the southern part of Ontario.

Population Map of Ontario, 2011

MANITOBA

ONTARIO

QUÉBEC

Legend
- · 1 dot represents 1000 people
- —— international border
- — province/territory border

N
W · E
S

1 cm = 170 km

Aamjiwnaang First Nation

London

Ella made connections to photos of two communities that she found. She noticed that in the photo of the Aamjiwnaang First Nation, the houses are spaced far apart. There are fewer dots in this area on the map. In the London photo, there are lots of houses. The map shows lots of dots in that area.

Aamjiwnaang First Nation

London

Try It

1 Use the steps for analyzing maps to look for another pattern on the population map.

2 Describe the pattern in your own words.

Land Use: Manufacturing

Manufacturing is the making of goods from materials, such as steel, plastic, and wood. The work can be done by people and machines. Sometimes, manufacturing is done in a factory. A **factory** is a place where people manufacture goods.

Many different types of manufacturing are done in this region. There are many roads, railroads, and large lakes and rivers for transporting materials and goods. This makes it easy to ship goods locally and around the world.

Workers put a propeller on an airplane at the Bombardier factory in Toronto.

Effects of Manufacturing

Manufacturing is important to this region and to all of Ontario. It provides work for people in this region. Some workers make goods. Other workers package goods. Then, different workers transport the goods to stores and warehouses.

Manufacturing provides goods that people need and want. These goods include cars, clothing, and vitamins.

Harmful chemicals are sometimes used in manufacturing. These chemicals can pollute the air, water, and soil. Companies must make sure that chemicals are used and stored safely.

As stewards of God's Creation, people can protect the land by buying only things they need. This cuts down on waste and pollution.

In Hamilton, companies have been manufacturing steel for more than 100 years.

I Wonder...

What connections are there between manufacturing and the common good?

Land Use: Farming

Interrelationships

Interrelationships are connections. Sometimes, these connections are between the environment and human activities. For example, the landform features of a region are connected to the types of work that people do there. As you read, ask yourself

- What connections do I notice?
- What positive and negative effects do I notice within these connections?

What connections are there between work done by farmers and other types of work?

The rich soil, flat land, and warm climate of this region are good for farming. Many different types of fruits, vegetables, and grains are grown there. For example, farms near Windsor grow corn and tomatoes. Farms near Hamilton and Niagara Falls grow fruits such as apples, peaches, and grapes. Farms near Kitchener raise animals, such as cows and chickens.

Effects of Farming

Farming creates many jobs. Some people work on the farms, planting and harvesting crops. Other people sell the crops and transport them.

Depending on the season, farm workers do different tasks. Here, farmers near Picton harvest pumpkins in fall.

When land is farmed for many years, the soil loses its nutrients to the plants. This makes it more difficult for things to grow. Sometimes, chemicals are used to keep the soil rich for plants. Adding these chemicals can sometimes damage the land and water in the area. Rain spreads chemicals into the soil, rivers, and lakes nearby.

Some farmers grow food without harmful chemicals. This process is called **organic farming**. Organic crops can be less damaging to the land.

Buying food that is grown locally can also help to protect the environment. When food does not have to be transported to distant places, less pollution from fuel is created.

One positive effect of people buying locally grown food is that they support farmers in their area.

Some farmers sell their products on the side of the road, or to stores and markets nearby. This woman is shopping at a farmer's market in Markham.

I Wonder...

How do growing populations in cities affect local farms and farmers?

Working in the Great Lakes–St. Lawrence Lowlands

Parmi
Geological Engineer
Kitchener

In my work, I test the soil and water in the city of Kitchener. I do this to make sure that human activities do not harm the land. We drill deep holes into the ground to do our tests. If I discover something wrong with the soil or water, I think of ways to clean them up. It makes me happy to help the environment in my work.

Brother Tom
Director of Shelter Services and Hospitality
Toronto

I work at a shelter for homeless men in Toronto. We serve 1100 meals a day and have beds for people who have nowhere to sleep. We are open every day of the year. We also provide clothing and counselling to people in the community. My favourite part of this job is helping people and seeing them succeed.

Darlene
Justice of the Peace
Gore Bay

I work as a justice of the peace in a small town. A justice of the peace is a type of judge. For my job, it is important that I listen to people telling their stories and make decisions based on facts. I make a difference in my community by being fair and upholding the law. I like to think that I help people and help to keep my community safe.

Evan
Director
Markham

I work as a director in Toronto. I travel there from my home in Markham. Directors make things like movies, TV shows, commercials, and music videos. I love working in the city because there are so many opportunities. Since many things are filmed in Toronto, we get new cameras and technology often. These help me do my job even better.

I Wonder...

How do different types of work serve the common good?

Comparing

Kitchener

Kitchener is a large city with a busy downtown. Many people work for technology companies and insurance companies. Other people work at universities and schools. Some people work at theatres and museums. Kitchener is surrounded by two other cities, as well as farmland.

Land Use: Homes

Kitchener has different types of homes to meet the needs of the people who live there. For example, people live in apartment buildings, seniors' homes, townhouses, and houses. Many homes are close to parks and schools.

Kitchener's downtown has apartments above some stores and restaurants. There are also tall apartment buildings, such as the one in the background.

Welcome to

Kitchener

Population: 219 153

Communities

Picton

Picton is a town in Prince Edward County. A **county** is a large area with many communities. Many tourists visit Picton for its theatres, festivals, and nearby sandy beaches. People in Picton work at different businesses, such as hotels and stores. The town is surrounded by farmland.

Land Use: Homes

In Picton, people live in houses close to the downtown area. Some people live in apartment buildings. Other people live in homes on the waterfront. Most stores are located in the downtown area.

Picton has a mix of older homes and newly built homes.

Welcome to

Picton

Population: 4487

I Wonder ...

How do these communities compare with my community?

Land Use: Conservation

When land is used for conservation, it is protected. The land is not used for other purposes, such as building homes and businesses. Forests, meadows, wetlands, lakes, and rivers are protected for the plants and animals that also live there.

Some conservation areas have trails and buildings for people who visit. Other conservation areas are left as natural areas.

Effects of Conservation

Some people work to care for conservation areas. Guides teach people how to respect and care for the environment. Scientists study the plants and animals there. They also study the effects that people's activities have on the plants and animals.

Visitors use a boardwalk to explore the wetlands at Point Pelee National Park. When visitors stay on boardwalks and trails, they avoid damaging plants and animals.

People can experience and learn about the environment in conservation areas. They can also use those areas for recreation, such as hiking and birdwatching. Natural resources are protected from people's activities.

Sometimes, conservation areas are located on land that was used for other purposes. An area that was once used for manufacturing can be replanted with trees. Over time, pollution in damaged wetlands can be cleaned up. Then, these areas become safe homes again for plants and animals.

Catholic Connection

Using land for conservation is one way that we care for God's Creation. Our Church teaches us to be responsible stewards of the environment.

These volunteers help scientists record the number of plants and animals along the Humber River in 2014. How can you help the environment?

I Wonder...

What can people do at conservation areas in my community?

Evaluate and Draw Conclusions

Should people take a bus instead of driving a car in my community?

When you evaluate, you identify the information that is most important to answer your inquiry question. When you draw conclusions, you make decisions or form opinions to answer your inquiry question. You use the evidence you found to support your conclusion.

Ella Investigates

Ella wondered about the effects on the environment if people take a bus instead of driving a car in her community of Ottawa. She reviewed the chart she had created.

Cars	Buses
Cars create road traffic.	There are special lanes for buses to get around road traffic.
Cars cause air pollution.	When you take buses, there are fewer cars on the road, so there is less pollution.
You can drive at any time. A car takes you directly where you want to go.	Travel time may be longer because you must wait for a bus and follow the bus route and schedule.
A car holds a small number of people.	A bus moves a lot of people at once.

Ella used the following questions to evaluate and draw conclusions:

Questions for Evaluating and Drawing Conclusions

- Do I have enough information to answer my inquiry question?
- What is most important in the information I collected?
- What conclusion can I draw based on the information?
- What evidence supports my conclusion?

Ella could see that she had a good amount of evidence to answer her inquiry question. She noticed that there were several negative things about driving cars, such as road traffic and air pollution.

Ella decided that the most important pieces of evidence she found were connected to pollution. She concluded that buses are the best option for the common good of the community. She noticed that the information about buses moving a lot of people at once supported this conclusion, too.

About 375 000 people ride Ottawa's buses and trains every day.

Try It

1. Review the different types of land use in this chapter.

2. Which land use do you think has the biggest effect on the environment?

3. Support your conclusion with evidence.

Making Decisions about Land Use

Communities consider the possible effects that land use may have on the environment. They also think about people's needs and wants. They consider questions such as these:

- Who will benefit from this land use?

- How does this land use affect the common good?

- Does the community need this land use?

This park is in Toronto. When communities decide to build new parks, they need to think carefully. Whose perspectives should be considered when parks are created?

I Wonder ...

What are some ways that communities can meet the needs of people while still caring for the land?

Working for the Common Good

Father Mike Says ...

To serve the common good, we need to remember two facts. First, God is the real owner of Earth. He lets us use it. Second, God wants us to use Earth so that it meets the needs of all people, present and future.

Why is it important to think about the common good in a community?

SEE

Think about how people work for the common good in the Great Lakes–St. Lawrence Lowlands.

REFLECT

What are some rules that I follow to support the common good?

ACT

Create a new rule for your classroom or school to support the common good.

What I Discovered

With a small group, discuss what you have discovered about the Great Lakes–St. Lawrence Lowlands. Next, discuss how this region compares to other regions in Ontario.

Making Connections

Why do you think people choose to live or work in your community?

Chapter Inquiry

Consider the Chapter Question: Why do people live and work where they do?

1 Gather and organize information from the chapter to help you answer this question.

2 Interpret and analyze the information you find.

3 Evaluate and draw conclusions about the information using the questions on pages 76 and 77.

Tourists come from all over the world to visit Niagara Falls.

Comparing Communities

Choose one Ontario community to compare with your own. On a map, identify which landform region of Ontario each community is located in.

In your comparison, explore some of the following ideas:

- how the people of each community use the land to meet their needs
- how the use of land and resources affect the environment
- how people live and work in these communities
- how people act as stewards of God's Creation in these communities

Ask Questions

Develop one or more inquiry questions to guide your investigation into how land and resources are used in the two communities. Check your questions using the criteria on page 28.

When I ask questions, my questions will
✔ be on topic
✔ be worded clearly
✔ need more than a "yes" or "no" answer

When I gather and organize, I will
✔ use sources I can trust
✔ keep information that is useful
✔ organize the information in a way that will help me understand it

Gather and Organize Information

Review the chapters that explore the landform regions of the communities you have chosen. You may also need to gather information from other sources. These could be brochures, books, or community websites. You may wish to create a graphic organizer to organize your information.

Interpret and Analyze Information

When I interpret and analyze, I will
✔ put the information into my own words
✔ look for patterns and connections
✔ state my new understanding

Reread the information that you have gathered and organized. Identify the main ideas in the information. Put the information into your own words. Look for patterns in the information. Make connections between the two communities. Think about the new understanding you have about the communities.

Evaluate and Draw Conclusions

Look at the information that you interpreted and analyzed. Think about whether you have enough information to answer your inquiry question. Use the information to draw conclusions you can support.

When I evaluate and draw conclusions, I will

✔ identify what is important

✔ make a decision or form an opinion to answer my inquiry question

✔ state my conclusion clearly, using evidence

Communicate

Decide what information you want to share. Think about the most effective way to present the information. You might create a brochure, poster, or digital presentation. Use visuals such as photos, maps, and graphic organizers. Share your findings with your class.

When I communicate, I will

✔ use words and visuals to present my findings

✔ present the information clearly to help other people understand it

✔ make the information interesting for my audience

Reflect on Your Learning

Ask yourself

• What were the three most important things I learned from this investigation?

• What has my investigation taught me about being a steward of God's Creation?

Early Communities in Canada

For thousands of years, Aboriginal peoples have lived in the place we call Canada. People from other countries began to move here hundreds of years ago. Aboriginal peoples and newcomers built communities that later became Canada.

Our Faith

The Bible says ...

66 Since God loved us so much, we also ought to love one another. 99

1 John 4:11 (NRSV)

Seven Communities in Early Canada, 1825

Lake Superior

Sault Ste. Marie

UPPER CANADA

Lake Michigan

Georgian Bay

Saugeen Peninsula (Bruce Peninsula)

Lake Huron

York (Toronto)

Queen's Bush settlement

N W E S

1 cm = 50 km*

* Each cm on this map represents 50 km on the ground.

Lake Erie

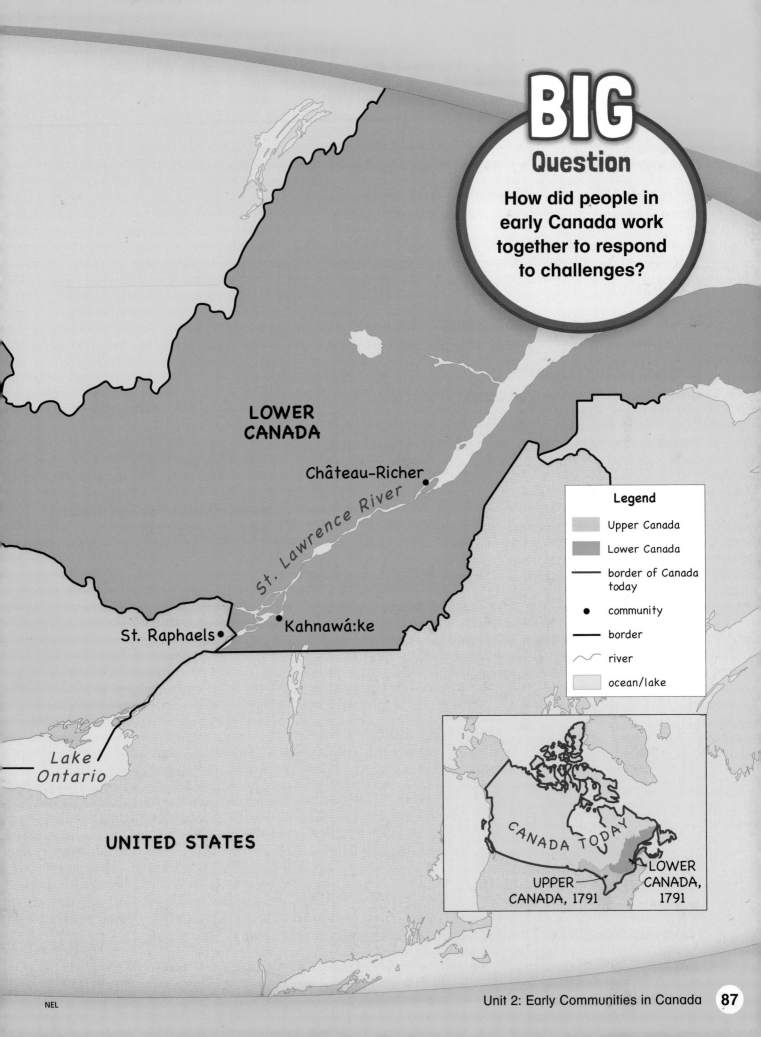

BIG

Question

How did people in early Canada work together to respond to challenges?

LOWER CANADA

Château-Richer

St. Lawrence River

St. Raphaels

Kahnawá:ke

Legend

Upper Canada

Lower Canada

border of Canada today

● community

border

~ river

ocean/lake

Lake Ontario

UNITED STATES

CANADA TODAY

UPPER CANADA, 1791

LOWER CANADA, 1791

Canada Long Ago

Long ago, Canada was very different from the Canada we live in today. In fact, it was not even called Canada. There were no paved roads, no stores, and no telephones. There were no cars or schools. Forests covered much of the land. Aboriginal peoples lived in communities where they farmed, hunted, and fished.

What we now call Canada began to change several hundred years ago. People started to come to Canada from other places. Some came on ships across a huge ocean. They came from France, England, Scotland, and Ireland. Others came on horses and on foot. They came from a place that would later be called the United States.

These people were called settlers. **Settlers** are people who build new communities.

England, Scotland, and Ireland were all part of Britain.

Sources of Some Settlers in Early Canada

UPPER LOWER
CANADA CANADA

UNITED STATES

FRANCE

❷

❸

❶

❶ ENGLAND
❷ SCOTLAND
❸ IRELAND

N
W E
S

1 cm = 1950 km

Legend

where many settlers came from

ocean/lake

Why Settlers Came

Settlers came for different reasons. Some settlers came for the chance to have land to farm. Some came because they did not feel safe where they lived. Some came for freedom. Some settlers came to be near other people who shared their language and faith.

New communities grew quickly. Some Aboriginal peoples had to move to other places because of the newcomers.

Understanding Canada Today

In early Canada, people spoke different languages and had different faiths. Over time, they built communities together. They learned how to respect one another. Understanding the history of these communities helps us understand Canada today.

This painting was created in 1838 by Philip John Bainbrigge. It shows a farm built by settlers in the thick forest of Upper Canada.

Early Communities

These images show seven communities in early Canada between 1780 and 1850. What do you notice?

By 1780, Mohawk people had been farming in Kahnawá:ke for many years.

By 1780, the French had been farming in Château-Richer for many years.

In 1784, Scottish settlers created the farming community of St. Raphaels.

By 1815, many Anishinabe people were living on the Saugeen Peninsula.

Around 1820, Black settlers escaped slavery and started a farming community in Queen's Bush.

In 1826, about 80 Métis families were living in the community of Sault Ste. Marie.

In 1834, the town of York got a new name: the city of Toronto.

Father Mike Says...

A home is a place where people feel welcome, treasured, and safe. Canada has new communities. We also have communities that have been here for thousands of years. We all need to work together to make this country a home for everyone.

Looking Ahead to the Unit Inquiry

At the end of this unit, you will be asked to create a guide for newcomers to early Canada. In it, you will give advice about how to meet the challenges of living in early Canada. You might give advice about how to do the following things:

- meet the needs for food, clothing, and shelter

- help each other

- grow a strong community

- act as stewards of God's Creation

At the end of the investigation, you will share your guide with your classmates.

Chapter 4

First Nations and Métis Communities

Our Faith

Jean Vanier said ...

66 Community is one of the most beautiful realities ... brothers and sisters loving and being together. 99

Essential Writings

Hi, I'm Nipa. I wonder: What was life like for people long ago?

In this chapter, you will

- identify three First Nations and Métis communities in Upper and Lower Canada
- ask questions
- compare the daily lives of people long ago
- reflect on how respect helps people work together in communities

How People Lived

These photos show objects that First Nations and Métis people were using around 1780. What do these objects tell you about how people lived?

porcupine-quill box

bone fishing hook

cow-horn rattle

stone arrowheads

leather moccasins

willow-reed ball

metal pot

Three Communities

Perspective

Perspective is how people see things. It is their point of view. People's perspectives depend on their beliefs and experiences. As you read, ask yourself

- What perspectives do I see?

- Whose perspectives are these?

- What is my perspective?

By 1780, First Nations peoples had been living in what we now call Canada for thousands of years. The forests, meadows, and waters provided everything they needed to live. They respected the environment.

Many newcomers had already arrived from France and Britain. They traded with First Nations people for fur. This was called the **fur trade**. They cut down trees to make farms.

Mohawk of Kahnawá:ke

The Mohawk are a First Nation. Long before 1780, Mohawk people were trading furs, such as beaver, with the British. The French wanted Mohawk people to trade furs with them, instead. They invited Mohawk people to settle near them, on the St. Lawrence River. Many agreed. They called their community *Kahnawá:ke*.

Three Communities, 1780

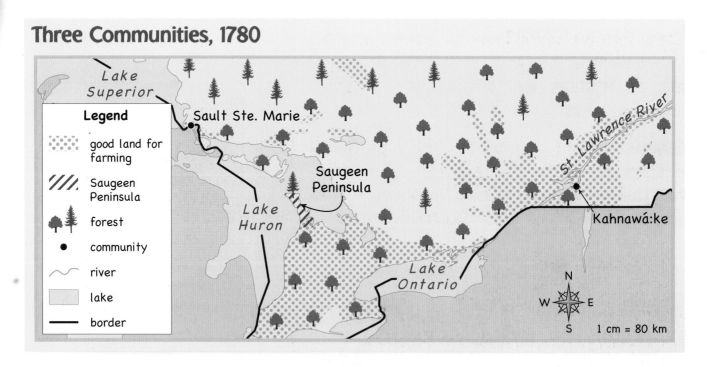

Legend

- good land for farming
- Saugeen Peninsula
- forest
- community
- river
- lake
- border

Lake Superior · Sault Ste. Marie · Saugeen Peninsula · Lake Huron · Lake Ontario · St. Lawrence River · Kahnawá:ke

1 cm = 80 km

Anishinabe in the Saugeen Peninsula

The Anishinabe are another First Nation. They lived in the forests around the big lakes called the Great Lakes. In 1780, British newcomers began to cut down forests in some areas. They drained marshes. They made farms. Some Anishinabe people lived on the Saugeen Peninsula. The land there still had a lot of forest. Other Anishinabe people came to live there, too.

Today, many Anishinabe people continue to gather resources from the land. This 2002 photo shows Richard McIvor and his daughter on Lake Wabigoon. They are collecting wild rice from the lake, as their ancestors did.

Métis of Sault Ste. Marie

Some First Nations women and French men in the fur trade started families together. Many years later, their children and grandchildren became known as **Métis**.

Some Métis people chose to live along a river that was part of a major fur-trading route. This area had good fishing and land that could be farmed. The community was called Sault Ste. Marie.

What perspectives on the environment do you see on these pages?

I Wonder...

What is my perspective on the environment?

Kahnawá:ke

In 1780, Kahnawá:ke was a Catholic community. Some Mohawk families lived in big longhouses. About 20 families might share one longhouse.

Mohawk Women

Mohawk women were powerful. They were in charge of the longhouses. They chose which men would make decisions for the community.

Women worked together. They supported their community by farming. They cared for the children. They prepared food so it would not spoil. They made clothing from animal skins.

By 1780, not all Mohawk people were living in traditional longhouses. Some were living in log cabins. What does this illustration tell you about how Mohawk people in Kahnawá:ke used the land to meet their needs?

smoke hole

longhouse

lacrosse stick

bone hoe

snowshoe

corn-husk dolls

NEL

Mohawk Men

Men worked together. They fished, hunted, and trapped. They built longhouses. Men made tools such as axes, bows, and arrows. They also made canoes and snowshoes.

Mohawk Children

Girls worked alongside the women. Boys worked alongside the men. Sometimes, children played with corn-husk dolls. Some played lacrosse.

Changing Ways of Life

Before coming to Kahnawá:ke, Mohawk people moved their whole community every few years. In Kahnawá:ke, they decided to stay in one place.

Beaver furs were very popular in the fur trade. For a long time, there were a lot of beavers. Mohawk trappers traded beaver furs for goods, such as sewing needles. By 1780, most of the beavers in the area had been trapped.

Catholic Connection

Kateri Tekakwitha was a Catholic Mohawk. She was a courageous and faithful follower of Jesus. In 1680, she died at the age of 24. In 2012, she was named a saint because of her remarkable faith and holiness. She is a patron saint of the environment.

people trading

woman pounding corn

log cabin

stretched hide

How did people build a strong community in Kahnawá:ke?

Saugeen Peninsula

In 1780, the Saugeen Peninsula was covered in forest. The soil was rocky. The Anishinabe people did not mind because they did not farm.

Family Life

Anishinabe people travelled the Saugeen Peninsula in family groups. They knew where to find fruit, like blueberries. They knew when streams were full of fish. They knew where to hunt deer, moose, and bear. In summer, they travelled by canoe. In winter, they pulled their belongings on toboggans.

Family members worked together. Children worked alongside their parents, who taught them how to live in the forest. Grandparents travelled with their families. Many grandparents were respected Elders. **Elders** are people who teach the skills, beliefs, and traditions of their community.

What does this illustration tell you about daily life in an Anishinabe community?

wigwam

birchbark box

woman cleaning a deerhide

Tools, Homes, and Clothing

Anishinabe people used birchbark for making baskets, dishes, cups, and canoes. Birchbark is strong and waterproof. Anishinabe people built wigwams. **Wigwams** are a type of home made from birchbark, fur, bulrush leaves, and wooden poles. They are sturdy and warm in wind and snow. Anishinabe women sewed moccasins and other clothing from leather.

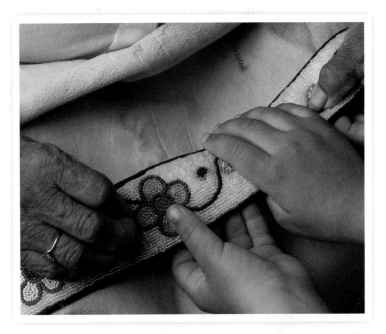

In this recent photo, an Anishinabe Elder teaches her granddaughter about Anishinabe beadwork. What makes Elders good teachers?

Changing Ways of Life

By 1800, Anishinabe people were getting many tools from newcomers. They traded fur for axes, blankets, traps, and pots. Some families began living in log cabins.

In 1836, the British and Anishinabe people made an agreement. The British said that newcomers would stay away from the Saugeen Peninsula. The newcomers came anyway. They cut down the trees and fished the lakes and rivers. It became difficult for the Anishinabe people to continue their traditional way of life.

I Wonder...

How did the community in the Saugeen Peninsula compare with the community in Kahnawá:ke?

Sault Ste. Marie

Métis people in Sault Ste. Marie built log cabins along the river, near a fur-trading post. By 1826, about 80 homes were there. The farms were close together because the Métis people liked to be near their neighbours.

The Métis people lived a life that combined the traditions of their First Nations and French ancestors. Most Métis people were Catholic. They spoke a Métis language called Michif. It combines French and Cree. Cree is a First Nations language.

Métis Women

Women took care of the farm and the family. They grew crops like beets, turnips, and corn. They gathered wild plants for food and medicine. They cleaned beaver furs for trading. Women made maple syrup and snowshoes. They also made clothes from moose or deer hide and cloth.

In Sault Ste. Marie, Métis families cleared long strips of land for farming. What does this illustration tell you about daily life in a Métis community?

playing a string game

weaving a sash

transporting furs and supplies

drying meat

cleaning moosehide

Métis Men

Many Métis men worked for fur-trading companies. They paddled large canoes full of furs or supplies to distant places. Métis men were sometimes away from home all summer. In winter, they trapped furs.

Men also hunted and fished. They supplied the fur-trading post at Sault Ste. Marie with meat and fish. They built canoes for the trading companies. In return, they received goods such as flour and sugar.

Métis Children

Children helped with the chores. They played games like tag. They learned from their Elders how to live in harmony with each other and the land. Elders also told them Gospel stories.

Faith in Action

In Superior North Catholic District School Board, students made books to celebrate the Métis people of Ontario. Students showed respect for Métis culture by contributing drawings, photos, and stories.

The Métis Culture

This sketch of a Métis dance was made in 1860. The Métis people had dances like this in Sault Ste. Marie. Their songs and dances combined French, Scottish, and First Nations traditions.

I Wonder ...

What connections can I make with the Métis of Sault Ste. Marie?

Ask Questions

Asking questions helps you find answers to things you wonder about. How can you create good inquiry questions?

Steps for Asking Inquiry Questions

1. Think about the topic. What do you already know? What do you want to learn?

2. Think of possible questions. Write them down.

3. Check each of the questions using criteria, such as the following:

   - A good question is on topic.
   - A good question is worded clearly.
   - A good question must be answered with more than a "yes" or "no."

I wonder how the lives of First Nations people changed around 1780.

Nipa Investigates

Nipa wondered how the lives of First Nations people changed in early Canada. She thought about the tools she could use to develop questions. She decided to use a 5W and H chart. She created questions using the words *who*, *what*, *where*, *when*, *why*, and *how*.

5W and H	My Questions
Who	Who were the First Nations heroes?
What	What did First Nations people do?
Where	Where did the British King live?
When	When did the lives of First Nations people begin to change?
Why	Why did newcomers take so much good land?
How	How did the lives of First Nations people change?

After making her chart, Nipa used the criteria in step 3 to decide if her questions were good.

Cornelius Krieghoff created this painting of First Nations people transporting furs in 1858.

Try It

1 Use the criteria in step 3 to judge Nipa's questions.

2 Which of Nipa's questions works best? Explain why you think it is the best question.

Shaping Canada

First Nations and Métis peoples are Aboriginal peoples of Canada. This means that they are among the first peoples of our land.

First Nations and Métis communities are found all across Canada today. Many place names come from First Nations languages. For example, *Oshawa* means "crossing of a stream" in a First Nations language called Seneca.

Every June 21, Canadians celebrate **National Aboriginal Day**. It is a day to honour Aboriginal peoples. It is our chance to celebrate together.

A young Mohawk dancer performs the shawl dance in Brampton. This photo was taken during National Aboriginal Day celebrations in June 2012.

I Wonder ...

How do celebrations in my community bring people together?

People Are Part of a Community

Father Mike Says ...

Pope Benedict said, "Openness to God makes us open toward our brothers and sisters." That is how different people can live side by side.

How do families work together in a community?

 SEE

Think about how the people in each community described in this chapter worked together.

 REFLECT

Why was it important for people in these communities to work together? Why is it important for people in your community to work together?

ACT

Share your ideas about the importance of working together with your family and friends.

What I Discovered

Draw a longhouse, a wigwam, and a log cabin. On each home, record one fact or idea you learned about the people in this chapter.

Chapter Inquiry

Suppose that you were moving to Canada around 1780. You could ask for advice from First Nations and Métis people.

1 Think about what you already know about living in early Canada. Think about what you still want to know.

2 Create questions using a chart like the one on page 105.

3 Test your questions against the criteria for a good inquiry question on page 104.

4 Choose one question that you want to investigate further.

Making Connections

Compare your life with the lives of children who lived in a First Nations or Métis community described in this chapter.

Kahnawá:ke

Saugeen Peninsula

Sault Ste. Marie

French Canadians in Château-Richer

Our Faith

Pope Benedict XVI said ...

" ... The human race is a single family. "

Charity in Truth, no. 53

> Hi, my name is Theo. I wonder: Why does a community grow the way it does?

In this chapter, you will

- identify why a community forms
- gather and organize information
- describe how Château-Richer helped shape Canada
- reflect on the ways people contribute to the common good

A French Canadian Community in 1800

What connections can
you make to this illustration?

How Château-Richer Formed

Château-Richer is a French Canadian community. In the 1600s, the king of France wanted more land. He sent French people to live in what is now Canada. They called this place New France. The French lived beside First Nations peoples in the area.

One new community in New France was Château-Richer. French settlers began to arrive there around 1640. The area had good farmland. There were many animals to trap. Settlers could sell their crops and furs. Château-Richer was one of the first Catholic parishes in New France.

At first, there were no roads joining communities. People settled close to the St. Lawrence River so they could travel by boat. In winter, they travelled on the frozen river by sleigh.

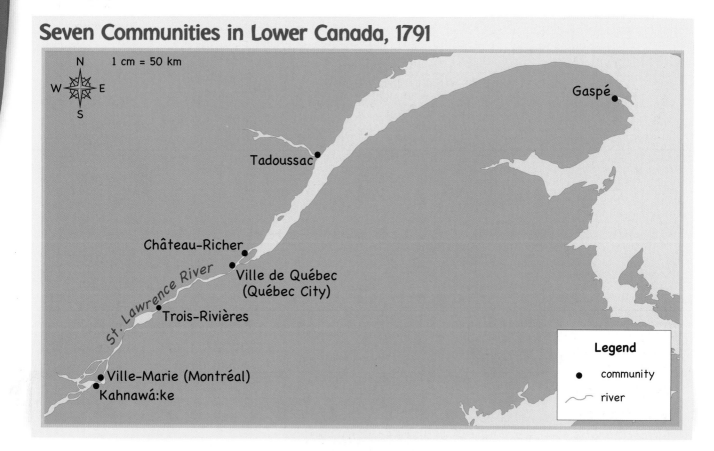

Seven Communities in Lower Canada, 1791

1 cm = 50 km

Gaspé

Tadoussac

Château-Richer

Ville de Québec (Québec City)

St. Lawrence River

Trois-Rivières

Ville-Marie (Montréal)

Kahnawá:ke

Legend
- community
~ river

Farming

People called **seigneurs** were in charge of big blocks of land called **seigneuries**. Seigneurs divided the seigneuries into long, thin farms. They assigned the farms to farmers called **habitants**. Château-Richer was a successful farming community.

French and British

By 1791, the British ruled New France. They renamed part of it Lower Canada. By this time, habitants had been living in Château-Richer for more than 100 years. The British wanted the habitants to stay. The habitants kept their language, culture, and religion.

Catholic Connection

The nuns of the Notre-Dame Congregation ran schools for girls. These were the first schools for girls in early Canada. One school was in Château-Richer. It was destroyed by the British in 1759. Later, in 1829, it was rebuilt.

shared land

farm house

road

barn

Thomas Davies created this painting of Château-Richer in 1787. What do you notice about the community and the land surrounding it?

I Wonder ...

What changed when the British began to rule New France?

Chapter 5: French Canadians in Château-Richer   **113**

Daily Life

In the 1800s, people in Château-Richer worked hard to survive. They could not buy things in a store. They had to grow their own food and make their own clothes. They chopped wood to heat their homes. Everyone helped harvest crops in fall.

First Nations people showed habitants how to make many things. For example, they showed habitants how to make maple syrup from the sap of the sugar maple tree in spring.

Habitant Women

- cared for children
- raised chickens and pigs
- milked cows
- grew vegetables, herbs, and flowers
- cooked and baked
- spun wool and made clothes

Habitant Men

- farmed in summer
- fished the river
- chopped firewood
- trapped animals in winter
- worked a few days each year on the seigneur's farm
- gave wheat and fish to the seigneur for the use of the land

Seigneur

- organized habitants to build and maintain roads, a grain mill, and a church
- ran a court for settling arguments
- collected fees from habitants for using the mill or fishing the river

Habitant Children

- weeded the vegetable garden
- brought firewood inside
- collected eggs
- picked berries in summer
- boys helped their fathers
- girls helped their mothers

Habitant Homes

Habitants' homes were made of logs covered in a white paste. They were built with steep roofs so the heavy snow would slide off. Most homes had one big room and an attic.

All homes had a big stone fireplace, and some homes had a wood stove. Homes had no electricity, no running water, and no refrigerator. People kept fruit and vegetables in a room under the floor. They slept on mattresses stuffed with straw or feathers.

The Church

The Catholic church was the centre of Château-Richer. Habitants attended Sunday Mass and went to social events at the church. They gave some of their money to support the church. Nuns ran schools for children.

Parish Priest

- organized help for people in need
- baptized babies
- taught people about their faith
- heard confessions
- witnessed marriages
- held funerals
- kept a record of the community

Nun

- taught girls about their faith
- taught girls reading, writing, mathematics, history, geography, and housework

I Wonder...

What would I like about living in Château-Richer in the 1800s? What would I dislike?

Gather and Organize Information

How did habitants use clothing to meet the challenges of winter in Château-Richer?

Steps for Gathering Information

① Think about the information you need.

② Identify sources you can use, for example, books and magazines, maps and other images, websites, and interviews.

③ Choose sources you can trust, such as nonfiction books and museum websites.

Theo Investigates

Theo thought about where to look for information about clothing worn by early French Canadians. He looked in nonfiction books and on websites.

Theo knew that he could trust this information because he found it on a government website.

Clothing Worn in Château-Richer

Women wore long dresses and skirts made out of wool, linen, or hemp. In winter, they wore shawls, scarves, and capes. In summer, they wore bonnets tied with a ribbon at the chin.

The men wore deerskin or moosehide jackets and pants with a leather belt. They wore a woolen hat called a *tuque*. This bright hat had a tassle at the tip.

To keep warm in winter, men and women wore woolen underwear, knit stockings, and leather moccasins. They lined their outer clothes with fur for extra warmth.

Steps for Organizing Information

1. Organize the information to help you understand it. Sort your information into categories by putting similar ideas together. Sometimes, it helps to use an organizer.

2. Check that you have enough information.

Theo Investigates

Theo thought about how to organize his information. He noticed that both men and women wore warm clothes in winter. However, some of their clothes were different. He decided to sort his information using a Venn diagram.

Winter Clothes for Women
- long dresses and skirts
- shawls, scarves, and capes

- woolen underwear
- knit stockings
- leather moccasins
- clothing lined with fur

Winter Clothes for Men
- animal skin jackets and pants
- leather belts
- woolen hats with tassles

Try It

1. Find six facts in this chapter to help you answer the following inquiry question: How did habitants meet the challenges of daily life in Château-Richer?

2. Sort your information by putting similar ideas together. You may wish to use an organizer.

What Was Significant in Château-Richer?

Significance

Significant means important. People, things, events, and places can all be significant. What is significant for one group may not be significant for another. As you read, ask yourself

- What is significant?
- Who is it significant to?
- Why is it significant?

You can tell what is significant to people by their actions.

Family

Habitants worked hard to support their families. Everyone worked together to make the things that their families needed. Most families were very large. The habitants saw children as God's gifts. Children were also a big help in getting all the work done.

Community

Habitants worked hard for the common good of the community, as well. For example, if a bridge needed repairs, they would work together to fix it. Everyone used the mill to grind their wheat into flour. If the mill needed repairs, everyone would help.

Cornelius Krieghoff painted *The Blizzard* in 1857. It shows a scene that happened often in Château-Richer. How might the habitants have helped one another?

Catholic Faith

Their Catholic faith helped the habitants feel like one big family. Their faith was an important part of life. The church encouraged people to help each other. For example, if a family had no food, a neighbour might bring over a meat pie or a hen.

Trade

In 1800, Anishinabe and Wendat people lived to the west of Château-Richer. Innu people lived to the northeast. People from these First Nations would sometimes share their knowledge of the land. They gave furs to habitants in return for goods, such as tools and blankets. Habitants sold the furs for money. The extra money helped them pay for things that their families needed.

Faith in Action

Julia was a student at Blessed Teresa of Calcutta Catholic Elementary School in Hamilton, Ontario. She knew that very sick people sometimes lose their hair. Julia wanted to help someone, so she cut off her hair. She gave it to a charity. The charity used the hair to make a wig for a sick child.

Why was trade significant?

Cornelius Krieghoff created this painting in 1848. It shows a habitant and two First Nations people in Lower Canada. What does this painting tell you about the relationship between habitants and First Nations people?

I Wonder ...

What do the actions of the habitants tell me about what was significant to them?

Shaping Canada

French Canadians influenced the country that Canada became. For example, many early Canadians spoke French. Later, Canada became a **bilingual country**. This means that we have two **official languages**: English and French.

This photo shows a parade in Québec City in 2005. It was part of the New France Festival. Every year, French Canadians celebrate their long history in Canada in this parade.

I Wonder...

What is the significance of French people coming to Canada?

Working for the Common Good

Father Mike Says ...

When we do our best to make our communities better, we help everyone to live better. We help the common good.

Why do people help each other?

SEE

How did the people of Château-Richer work for the common good?

REFLECT

Think about some examples of people working for the common good in your community.

ACT

Decide on one way that you can help your community. Act on your idea.

What I Discovered

Cut out one long strip of paper. In the middle of the paper, write one significant fact or idea about life in Château-Richer in the 1800s. Draw a habitant farm around your writing.

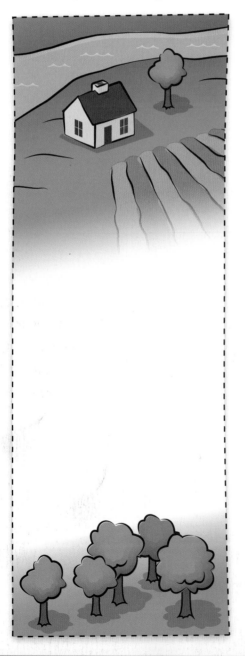

Making Connections

How is your life the same as the lives of children in Château-Richer? How is it different?

Chapter Inquiry

1 Think about the chapter inquiry question: Why does a community grow the way it does?

2 Gather five pieces of information from the chapter to help you answer this question.

3 Use a chart or another organizer to help you sort your information.

Scottish Newcomers in St. Raphaels

Our Faith

The Bible teaches ...

No community grows without people who work hard and work well.

Adapted from Sirach 38:31–32

> Hi, my name is Sierra. I wonder: What relationship did Scottish newcomers have with their environment?

In this chapter, you will

- describe how people in St. Raphaels affected the environment

- interpret and analyze information

- compare people's roles in the past and present

- compare challenges in the past and present

- reflect on how people work together to build community

A Day on the Farm

These scenes show a day in the life of Scottish settlers. Spot how this family used the environment.

5 a.m.

7 a.m.

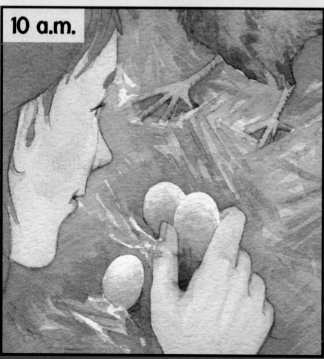

10 a.m.

12 p.m.

2 p.m.

4 p.m.

6 p.m.

8 p.m.

Chapter 6: Scottish Newcomers in St. Raphaels

How St. Raphaels Formed

St. Raphaels is a small farming community. It was formed by two groups of Scottish settlers: Loyalists from the United States and farmers from Scotland.

In 1783, settlers in the United States had just won a war with Britain. People who had fought on the British side had to leave the United States. They found safety in Upper Canada. They were called **Loyalists** because they were loyal to Britain.

One group of Scottish Loyalists started a community together in 1784. It was later called St. Raphaels.

Meanwhile, in Scotland, there was not enough land for everyone. Some farmers heard that the British government was offering land in St. Raphaels. They decided to move. In 1785 and 1786, 800 Scottish farmers came to St. Raphaels.

C.W. Jefferys created this illustration for a book published in 1945. It shows settlers clearing land in Upper Canada in 1830. Why would neighbours help each other with this task?

St. Raphaels in Upper Canada, 1800

Legend

→ Scottish Loyalists arriving from the United States in 1784

→ Scottish settlers arriving from Scotland in 1785 and 1786

— border

LOWER CANADA

• Montréal (Ville-Marie)

St. Raphaels

Cornwall

UPPER CANADA

St. Lawrence River

Akwesasne (St. Regis)

Kingston

York (Toronto)

Lake Ontario

UNITED STATES

N W E S

1 cm = 40 km

Almost all the settlers in St. Raphaels were Scottish Catholics. They spoke a language called Gaelic. The British government gave them land, tools, and seeds.

Working Together

First Nations people near St. Raphaels helped the Scottish people adjust to life in Upper Canada. For example, Mohawk people showed them how to make canoes.

The farmers from Scotland did not know how to change forests into farmland. The Scottish Loyalists showed their new neighbours what to do.

I Wonder ...

What challenges would each group of Scottish newcomers have had in St. Raphaels?

Challenges

The Environment

When the Scottish settlers arrived, dense forest covered the land. To make farm fields, they used axes to chop down the trees. They moved rocks and boulders out of the way. It was hard work.

There were no stores in St. Raphaels. Settlers had to make almost everything they needed. They used materials from the environment. They used wood to build their homes, furniture, wagons, and wheelbarrows. They used rocks to build fireplaces and fences.

Settlers grew all their own food. Mohawk people showed them how to grow corn, beans, squash, and pumpkins together. Settlers also grew cucumbers, cabbages, and wheat. It could take a few years before a farm provided enough food to feed a family. People were often hungry.

In this photo, a man demonstrates how settlers in Upper Canada plowed a field if they had horses. *Plowing* means digging through the soil. Plants grow more easily in loosened soil.

Most houses had one large room with a big fireplace. In winter, settlers added wood to the fire all day long to keep the house warm. To wash dishes or cook, they carried water in buckets from a stream or well. In winter, they melted ice on the fire for water. For light, they burned candles they made from animal fat.

On Their Own

Newcomers often felt **isolated**, or lonely. The farmhouses in St. Raphaels were far apart. There was no mail delivery. The telephone and Internet had not yet been invented. People felt very far away from friends and family in Scotland. Over time, they made friends with their neighbours. They saw each other when they went to church on Sunday.

Faith in Action

At St. Thérèse of Lisieux Catholic Elementary School in Hamilton, Ontario, Grade 3 students collected mittens, hats, and scarves. Then, they donated these items to people who were homeless in their community to help the people stay warm.

In these photos, children demonstrate the work of settler children. How do you help your family?

I Wonder ...

If I were a newcomer in St. Raphaels, what would be most challenging for me?

Daily Life

Women and Girls

In St. Raphaels, women and girls had busy days. They spent their time cleaning, dyeing, and spinning sheep's wool. They wove the wool to make cloth and blankets. They sewed clothing and knitted socks and mittens. They cooked and baked. They washed clothes in large tubs of water. Women and girls also milked cows and collected eggs. They worked with the men and boys to harvest crops in fall.

Men and Boys

Men and boys planted crops in spring. They cut down trees for firewood and for building. They hunted animals. Some looked after cows, sheep, or pigs, if they owned any. Settlers did not have refrigerators. To make meat last, men packed it into barrels with salt.

In this photo, a woman demonstrates how settlers in Upper Canada spun wool. Spinning was just one step in the long process of turning wool into warm clothing.

In this photo, a man demonstrates how settlers in Upper Canada made planks. Planks are flat pieces of wood. They can be used to make wagons, tables, and benches.

The Church

The community's first priest was Father Alexander Macdonell. He helped the settlers build a small wooden church just a few years after they arrived. They called it the Blue Chapel because it had a blue ceiling. The church helped to connect everyone in the community.

The priest was an important figure in St. Raphaels. He baptized children and performed marriage ceremonies. He gave comfort and advice.

Later, St. Raphaels had another priest called Father Alexander McDonell. In 1819, he helped replace the Blue Chapel with a large stone church. He called it St. Raphaels.

Catholic Connection

Father Alexander McDonell built three schools in St. Raphaels. There was a school for boys, a school for girls, and a school to train new priests. These were among the very first Catholic schools in Upper Canada. After he became a bishop, Father McDonell helped to set up new parishes throughout Upper Canada.

This 1823 painting by Martin Archer Shee shows Father Alexander McDonell. In 1826, Father McDonell became the first Catholic bishop of Upper Canada.

I Wonder...

How did the lives of children in St. Raphaels compare with the lives of First Nations and Métis children long ago?

Interpret and Analyze Information

To investigate a topic, you need to interpret and analyze information.

- **Interpreting** means understanding information and putting it in your own words.
- **Analyzing** means digging deeper. You take information apart to help you understand it.

Steps for Interpreting and Analyzing Information

1. Put the information into your own words. You may wish to organize your information to help you think about it.

2. Think about what your information means. Look for patterns and connections.

3. State your new understanding.

What knowledge did First Nations people share with newcomers?

Sierra Investigates

Sierra was investigating the advice that First Nations people gave to newcomers in early Canada. After gathering some information, she wrote it down in her own words. She organized the information in a chart to help her analyze it.

What knowledge did First Nations people share with newcomers?

Food	Transportation	Medicine
how to collect sap from maple trees to make maple syrup	how to make canoes from birch bark	where to find honey to soothe sore throats
how to know which wild berries were safe to eat and which were poisonous	how to make snowshoes from wood and leather for travelling in deep snow	how to use cedar leaves to make tea with vitamin C
how to hunt and trap animals in new ways		
how and why to plant corn, beans, and squash together		

Sierra looked for patterns. She thought about how pieces of information connected to one another. After analyzing her chart, Sierra's new understanding was that First Nations people helped newcomers in a lot of different ways.

Try It

1. Reread page 130 to answer this inquiry question: How did the work of women and girls compare with the work of men and boys?

2. Follow the steps on page 132 to help you interpret and analyze the information.

Then and Now

Continuity and Change

Continuity means that things stay the same. **Change** means that things become different. As you read, ask yourself

- What changed over time?
- What stayed the same or did not change?

Until the 1840s, St. Raphaels was the largest Catholic parish in Upper Canada. Since then, many places in Canada have grown. St. Raphaels has not. It is still a small farming community. Local places still have their original Scottish names, like Glen Roy Road and Loch Garry.

Today, many Canadians have Scottish ancestors. Some Canadian families are related to the farmers who built the Blue Chapel. Many of these families still live near St. Raphaels.

What has changed in St. Raphaels? What has stayed the same?

People celebrate their Scottish heritage at the Glengarry Highland Games. These games are held near St. Raphaels.

I Wonder...

What has changed and what has stayed the same in my community?

People Are Part of a Community

Father Mike Says ...

When people work hard together, they create a community in two ways. First, they build homes, roads, stores, schools, and churches or other places of worship. Second, they create a feeling that together they are one.

What can we create by working together?

 SEE

Identify three ways that Scottish people worked hard to make a home and community in St. Raphaels.

 REFLECT

Think about the chores you do at home. How do your chores help you feel like part of your family?

ACT

What is your dream to help your community grow stronger? Think of one thing you could do to help. Act on it.

What I Discovered

Create a cycle diagram to show how the lives of the Scottish settlers changed each season. You can include both images and labels.

Making Connections

Canadians with Scottish ancestors still continue Scottish traditions, such as the Glengarry Highland Games. What connections can you make to this idea?

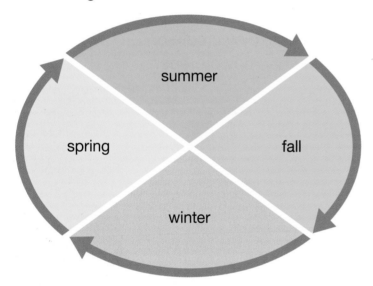

Chapter Inquiry

Consider this inquiry question: How did Scottish newcomers to St. Raphaels interact with the environment?

1 Gather information from the chapter. You can use other sources, too. Put the information into your own words. You may wish to organize your information to help you think about it.

2 Think about what the information means. Look for patterns and connections.

3 State your new understanding.

Black Settlers in the Queen's Bush Settlement

Our Faith

The Bible says ...

" ... Love your neighbour as yourself. "

Mark 12:31 (NRSV)

Hi, my name is Tiah. I wonder: How did settlers show respect for one another?

In this chapter, you will

- describe relationships between different communities in Canada
- identify examples of conflict and cooperation in the Queen's Bush settlement
- analyze maps
- compare people's daily lives long ago
- reflect on why we should care for and respect one another

Good Neighbours

This illustration shows a scene from the Queen's Bush settlement in 1840. What examples of cooperation do you see?

A New Home

Fleeing to Upper Canada

Before 1819, there was slavery in both Upper Canada and the United States. **Slavery** means that one person is the property of another person. Many Black people were prisoners of slavery.

In Upper Canada, slavery began to be discouraged. In 1819, all Black people in Upper Canada were declared free. Many people felt that slavery was wrong. Some of them helped others escape from slavery. They guided people escaping slavery north on the Underground Railroad. This was not a real railroad. It was a secret route.

Many Black people in the United States came to Upper Canada. It was a long way, but they wanted to be free.

Charles T. Webber painted *Underground Railroad* in 1893. In the painting, people who are fleeing slavery have just arrived at a house. Here, they will receive food and a bed for the night.

Getting Started

Some of the Black newcomers to Upper Canada wanted to farm, but they had no money to buy land. They heard about a vast wilderness called the Queen's Bush. Many Black settlers decided to farm there. They travelled into the forest and began to make their farms.

Several white families were already farming in the area. Some of them disagreed with slavery. They helped the newcomers get started. They loaned the Black settlers tools and gave them seeds. They hired Black settlers to help with the harvest. The farming community grew quickly. It became known as the Queen's Bush settlement.

People in slavery cannot

- attend school
- decide where to live
- choose their work
- earn money
- choose the person they want to marry
- keep their children

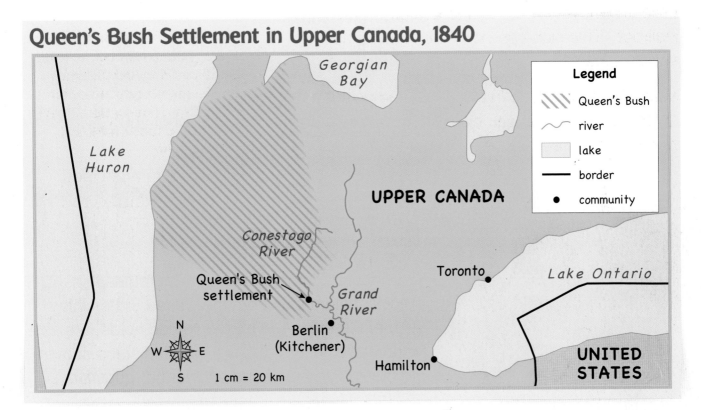

Queen's Bush Settlement in Upper Canada, 1840

I Wonder...

How did the actions of Black settlers show that freedom was important to them?

To sell crops or buy supplies was a two-day trip to Berlin. Berlin was a large community that was closest to the Queen's Bush settlement. Today, Berlin is called Kitchener.

Chapter 7: Black Settlers in the Queen's Bush Settlement **141**

Analyze Maps

Maps can show where things are in relation to each other. When you analyze something, you look at its parts and try to make sense of it.

Steps for Analyzing Maps

1. Read the title of the map. The title tells you the map's purpose.

2. Look at the other features of the map: scale, compass rose, legend, and notes. What information do the features give you?

3. Ask yourself questions about the map. What connections can you make? What patterns do you see? How does the information fit with what you already know?

4. Identify what you learned from the map.

Tiah Investigates

Tiah found a map showing some routes that Black settlers took from the United States into Upper Canada. The map also had notes with extra information. She followed the steps above to analyze the map and answer her question.

Why did Black communities form where they did in Upper Canada?

Some Destinations on the Underground Railroad, 1830–1850

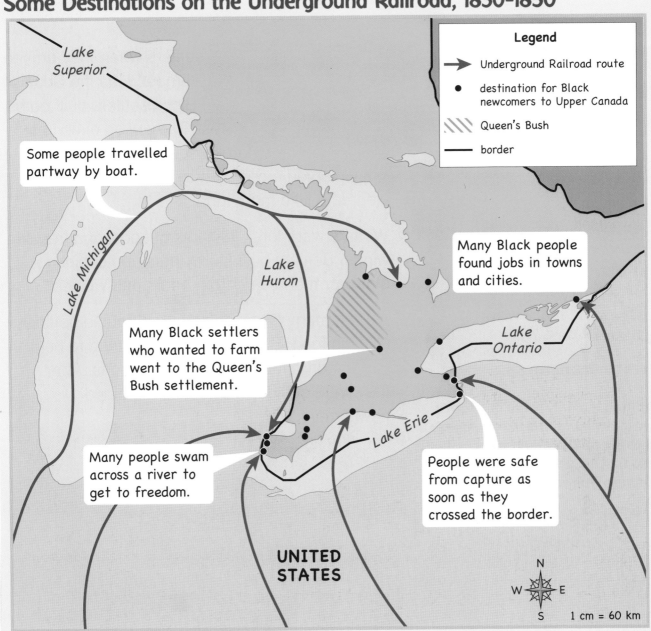

Legend

→ Underground Railroad route

• destination for Black newcomers to Upper Canada

▨ Queen's Bush

— border

Lake Superior

Some people travelled partway by boat.

Lake Michigan

Lake Huron

Many Black people found jobs in towns and cities.

Lake Ontario

Many Black settlers who wanted to farm went to the Queen's Bush settlement.

Lake Erie

Many people swam across a river to get to freedom.

People were safe from capture as soon as they crossed the border.

UNITED STATES

N W E S

1 cm = 60 km

Try It

1. Follow the steps on page 142 to analyze the map on this page.

2. What new questions do you have about the Underground Railroad?

Daily Life

Interrelationships

Interrelationships are connections. People can be connected with other people. People can also be connected with nature. As you read, ask yourself

- What connections do I notice?

- What positive and negative effects do I notice within these connections?

Life was hard for Black settlers when they arrived at the Queen's Bush settlement. Like the Scottish settlers in St. Raphaels, Black settlers built paths through the dense forest. They used axes to cut down trees. They broke up the soil with hoes. They planted crops by hand. Every year, they cleared a little more land.

Winters were long, with lots of snow and freezing winds. Settlers built sturdy huts and cabins to stay warm and safe from bears and wolves.

At first, many Black settlers had trouble getting enough food. Some white settlers tried to help. They shared their potatoes and beans. After they were settled, Black settlers helped newcomers, too.

At first, the only route into farms was a walking trail like the one in this photo. Over time, settlers built roads. This photo of a southern Ontario trail was taken in 2006.

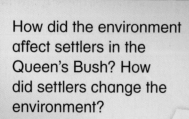

How did the environment affect settlers in the Queen's Bush? How did settlers change the environment?

A Community Grows

By 1840, up to 2000 Black settlers were living in the Queen's Bush settlement. It was the largest Black community in Upper Canada.

People built schools and churches to strengthen their community. Families went to church on Sundays. Churches held community events. Every year, August 1 was Emancipation Day. It was a day for celebrating freedom from slavery.

There were problems in the community, however. For example, Black people who worked in logging camps were paid less than other workers. Also, some white settlers did not want their children going to school with Black children.

As the years went by, life slowly got better for the Black settlers. They had food to eat and wheat to sell. Black and white farmers lived and worked side by side.

In church, people are connected to one another. For example, they support one another in difficult times.

Catholic Connection

Every community grows stronger when people work together and treat each other with respect. The Bible tells us how to do this. It says "love your neighbour as yourself."

This school in Waterloo was built in 1820. The schools in the nearby Queen's Bush settlement were similar. How does this school compare with yours?

I Wonder...

What interrelationships helped the Queen's Bush settlement grow?

Shaping Canada

Faith in Action

Students hold a multicultural parade every year at St. John Bosco Catholic School in Toronto, Ontario. Through the parade, students show their respect for everyone's culture.

These students attend Our Lady of Wisdom Catholic School in Toronto. This 2013 photo shows them celebrating Black History Month.

The settlers in the Queen's Bush settlement built farms on land owned by the government. In the 1840s, the government decided to sell the land. Only a few Black settlers could afford to buy their own farms from the government. The rest of the settlers lost everything.

The original Black families of this area were almost forgotten. Historians and writers have worked hard to help us remember them. As a result, we know about the Queen's Bush settlement. We know that people with different cultures lived together peacefully. Today, we call this multiculturalism. **Multiculturalism** means that people from all cultures can live together in dignity and have respect for one another.

I Wonder...

Why is it important to remember the history of Black settlers?

People Have Dignity

Father Mike Says ...

People are special among all the creatures on this Earth because we can know and speak to God. One of the ways that we show our love for God is by treating every person with respect.

Why is it important to treat people with respect?

 SEE

In what ways did people treat one another with respect in the Queen's Bush settlement?

REFLECT

Why do you think it is important to show respect to everyone?

 ACT

Think of one person you respect. Make a card for her or him explaining why.

Pulling It Together

What I Discovered

Think about what you learned in this chapter. Share

- three things you learned
- two things you found interesting
- one thing you would still like to learn about

Making Connections

In this chapter, you learned how settlers helped one another meet challenges. Who helps you meet challenges? How do you help other people meet challenges?

Chapter Inquiry

How could a map like the one below be helpful to someone who was moving to Upper Canada? Follow the steps on page 142 to analyze the map and answer this inquiry question.

Many of the roads in Upper Canada followed routes that First Nations people traditionally travelled.

Main Roads in Upper Canada before 1850

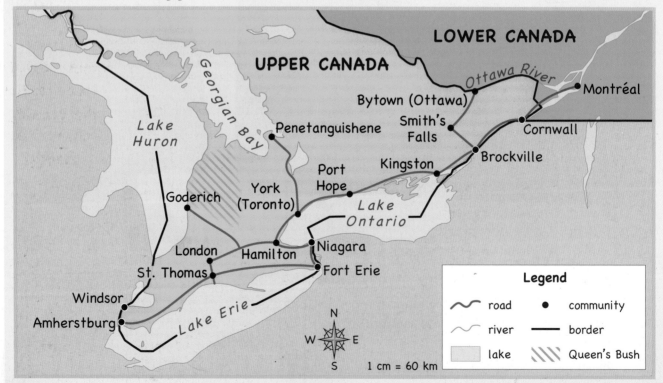

Newcomers Build Toronto

Our Faith

Pope Francis said ...

❝ ... To love God and neighbour ... means seeing in every person the face of the Lord. ❞

Hi, my name is Emmitt. I wonder: How did growing communities change?

In this chapter, you will

- describe challenges Toronto faced
- evaluate and draw conclusions
- compare people's roles in the past and present
- compare challenges people faced in the past and present
- reflect on why people care for those in need

A Growing Community

These two paintings show the same Toronto waterfront 50 years apart. What is the same? What is different?

Town of York, 1804

This painting shows the town of York on the shores of Lake Ontario. Elizabeth Hale painted this scene in 1804.

York became the city of Toronto in 1834. Edwin Whitefield painted this scene in 1854.

A New Town

Cause and Consequence

A **cause** is something that makes an event happen. A **consequence** happens as a result of that event.

As you read, ask yourself

- What caused the event to happen?

- What was the result, or consequence, of the event?

- Who was affected by it?

For many years, the people of the Mississauga First Nation hunted, fished, and traded where Toronto now stands. They knew the area as Tkaronto. *Tkaronto* means "where trees stand in the water."

After a war with the United States, the British wanted to build a fort. They made an agreement with the Mississauga First Nation to use the land at Tkaronto.

This location was across a big lake, away from the United States. At the fort, soldiers could protect Upper Canada from the United States. The British built the fort in 1793. They named it Fort York.

The building of Fort York was an event. A war caused that event. A new town was a consequence of the building of the fort.

Lieutenant Sempronius Stretton painted this scene of Fort York in 1804.

Loyalist Settlements in Upper Canada, 1815

Legend
- area with Loyalist settlement
- • community
- — border
- lake

Lake Huron

Georgian Bay

LOWER CANADA

UPPER CANADA

New Johnstown (Cornwall)

Elizabethtown (Brockville)

St. Lawrence River

Smith's Creek (Port Hope)

Kingston

York (Toronto)

Grand River

Lake Ontario

Hamilton

Dover Mills (Port Dover)

UNITED STATES

Sandwich (Windsor)

Lake Erie

N S E W

1 cm = 50 km

The Community Grows

The war had many consequences. Loyalists who had fought for the British needed to find safety. Many of them fled north to Upper Canada. For safety, many Loyalists settled around Fort York. This became the town of York.

Within a few years, York had homes, churches, government buildings, a market, and shops. It became an important centre.

Soon, other newcomers came to York hoping to find work or get land. Black people escaping slavery came from the United States. Other people travelled by boat from England, Scotland, and Ireland. Many newcomers chose York so that they could be part of a busy, growing community.

Between 1815 and 1850, York grew from a town of 720 people to a city of more than 30 000.

The people of the Mississauga First Nation were affected by York's growth. They could not keep living there in their traditional way. They moved to an area between the Grand River and Dover Mills.

I Wonder ...

What were some other causes of York's fast growth?

Chapter 8: Newcomers Build Toronto **153**

Daily Life

Types of Work in Early Toronto

- dressmaker
- government worker
- baker
- cook
- horse-carriage driver
- servant
- glass-blower
- map-maker

By 1834, the town of York was big enough to be called a city. People liked its original name, so they renamed the city *Toronto*.

The muddy streets of Toronto were crowded with people on horses, in carriages, and on foot. People bought food at the farmer's market. They visited shops to buy other goods, such as hats, candy, pottery, and newspapers. They went to the theatre. On Sunday, they went to church.

Toronto was busy and exciting. People came to visit the city from all over. In Toronto, people could sell their crops and buy supplies. They could also mail letters and put their money in the bank. Most smaller communities had few stores and no banks.

This drawing was created by W.H. Bartlett in 1840. It shows a Toronto fish market. People visited the docks to buy fresh fish, caught in Lake Ontario.

People Who Were Rich

In 1834, some people in Toronto had a lot of money. Some of them ran businesses. Some people worked for the government, the courts, or the bank. People who were rich owned land. They lived in big houses and wore expensive clothes. Servants cooked their meals and cleaned their homes. People who were rich could afford to pay for teachers for their children.

People Who Were Poor

Most newcomers had little money. Their lives were hard. They took whatever work they could find. Some found work building roads, bridges, and buildings. Others found work in factories and on nearby farms.

Both women and children worked as servants. Some made, washed, and cleaned clothes. Often, children sold newspapers or shined shoes on the streets. Toronto had no daycares. Many children looked after younger siblings while their parents worked.

Catholic Connection

Francis Collins was an Irish Catholic. He moved from Ireland to Toronto in 1818, when he was only 17 years old. He started a newspaper called the *Canadian Freeman*. In his newspaper, he spoke out against greed and unfairness.

In winter, people in Toronto had fun on frozen Lake Ontario. John Howard painted this scene, called *Taylor's Wharf, 1835*.

I Wonder ...

What connections can I make to the lives of people in early Toronto?

A Growing City

Challenges

City life in early Toronto was very different from city life today. Flush toilets and running water did not exist.

The city did not collect garbage. Instead, most people threw their garbage onto the streets or into nearby streams. Dirty water from the streams drained into Lake Ontario. People could get very sick when they drank water from the lake.

Many newcomers hoped to find work. Some could not find any. At first, Toronto's government did not feel that it was responsible for helping people in need. Seniors, people without work, and people with disabilities had to depend on their families for help. Some people begged in the streets for money or food.

This illustration shows a poor neighbourhood in early Toronto. Families lived in crowded one-room apartments. People took turns sleeping in the same bed. Their homes were drafty, dirty, and unhealthy.

Solving Problems

Some people in Toronto tried to solve the city's problems. Here are a few examples:

- In 1820, a group of women raised money. They gave it to pregnant women who could not afford healthcare.

- In 1837, the government built a home for people who could not support themselves. People who were frail or sick or had a disability could live there. Children did, too. Everyone in the home had to work for their meals and shelter.

- Around 1845, many Irish people who were poor arrived in Toronto. The Catholic Church gave them meals and places to sleep.

- Volunteer firefighters were ordinary people who were willing to help others. Most buildings in early Toronto were made of wood. They were heated by fireplaces. As a result, buildings often caught on fire.

Faith in Action

Morgan is a student at Thomas D'Arcy McGee Catholic School in Ottawa, Ontario. One day, he went to the grocery store with his mother. He saw a man asking for change. When he got home, Morgan got his birthday money. He went back to the store with his mother and gave the man his birthday money.

I Wonder ...

Why was it important for people in early Toronto to help each other?

Evaluate and Draw Conclusions

Steps for Evaluating

When you evaluate, you identify the information that is most important to answer your inquiry question.

1. Read the information you have gathered.

2. Identify what is important.

Steps for Drawing Conclusions

When you draw conclusions, you make decisions or form opinions to answer your inquiry question.

1. Check that you have enough information to answer your inquiry question.

2. Make a decision or form an opinion to answer your inquiry question. Support your answer with evidence.

3. State your conclusion clearly.

Emmitt Investigates

Emmitt gathered information about health and comfort in early Toronto. He organized it using the chart on the next page. Then, he followed the steps to evaluate and draw a conclusion.

Was health or comfort the biggest challenge in early Toronto?

HEALTH: Reasons why it was hard to be healthy in Toronto.	COMFORT: Reasons why it was hard to be comfortable in Toronto.
• Waste water and sewage polluted the streets. • Drinking dirty water made people sick. Some people died. • Many people did not have enough food. • Visiting the doctor cost a lot of money. • Doctors did not know how to cure most harmful illnesses. Some people died. • Garbage lay in the street. So did dead horses, dogs, and cats.	• Some people lived in crowded one-room apartments. In summer, the apartments were very hot. In winter, they were very cold. • Many people did not own warm winter clothes. • Mosquitoes from nearby swamps bothered most people. • People walked in muddy streets.

Emmitt noticed the "Health" column had more serious consequences than the "Comfort" column. He also noticed that many people died from reasons connected to health. He thought this information was important.

Emmitt decided he had enough information to answer his inquiry question. He concluded that being healthy was a more serious challenge than being comfortable in early Toronto.

Try It

1. Review the information on page 157. Identify ways that people tried to solve problems in early Toronto.

2. Which of these solutions most closely demonstrates the Our Faith quotation on page 149? To decide, follow the steps for evaluating and drawing conclusions on page 158.

Then and Now

Toronto has changed since the early 1800s. Today, it is the biggest city in Canada. It has garbage collection and schools. It has housing and services for people in need. Toronto is home to a large zoo, a science centre, and one of the tallest towers in the world. However, it also has new problems, like traffic jams.

Some things have stayed the same. People still rush around the city streets, to shop and get to work. Just like before, many people living in Toronto were born elsewhere. Visitors still come from far and wide. People living in Toronto still try to help others.

This photo shows a busy Toronto street in 2014. Compare this photo with other images of Toronto in the chapter.

I Wonder ...

Why do we all have a responsibility to solve problems in our communities?

Caring for People in Need

Father Mike Says ...

Pope Francis tells us that we must not just give food and clothes to people who are poor. We must also try to change the world so that people will no longer be poor.

How can we help people in need?

SEE

Where do you see people in your community needing help?

REFLECT

How would you change the world?

ACT

Discuss with your family ways that you could help people in need. Choose one action. Make it happen.

Pulling It Together

What I Discovered

The town of York went through many changes as it grew into the city of Toronto. Write down five changes. Sort those changes into categories such as population, transportation, and housing.

Chapter Inquiry

In early Canada, some people lived in cities. Other people lived on farms. Did city life or farm life in early Canada have more challenges?

1. Gather information about life in a city and life on a farm in early Canada. Farm life is described in Chapters 4, 5, 6, and 7. City life is described in this chapter. Organize your information to help you interpret and analyze it.

2. Follow the steps for evaluating and drawing conclusions on page 158.

Making Connections

All communities change. Ask an older family member or neighbour to tell you about how and why your community has changed.

St. Paul's Basilica Parish was the first Catholic church in Toronto. The original church was built in 1824. St. Paul's has a long history of helping people in need. This 1999 photo shows people celebrating the work of the parish.

Creating a Guide for Newcomers

Investigate the challenges people faced in Canada between 1780 and 1850, as well as the solutions they found. You will use this information to create a guide with advice for newcomers to early Canada. You might give advice about how to do the following things:

- meet the needs for food, clothing, and shelter

- help each other

- grow a strong community

- act as stewards of God's Creation

If you wish, you may focus on one community or one time period.

Ask Questions

Develop questions to guide your inquiry. Your questions should help you develop good advice for a newcomer to early Canada. You may want to create a chart to help you develop questions.

When I ask questions, my questions will

✔ be on topic

✔ be worded clearly

✔ need more than a "yes" or "no" answer

Unit Inquiry

When I gather and organize, I will

- ✔ use sources I can trust
- ✔ keep information that is useful
- ✔ organize the information in a way that will help me understand it

Gather and Organize Information

Review this unit to find information about challenges that people faced in early Canada. You may also gather information from other sources. Identify the solutions that people found.

Then, organize your information in a way that will help you understand it. For example, you might create a Venn diagram, an idea web, or a chart.

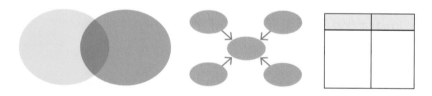

When I interpret and analyze, I will

- ✔ put the information into my own words
- ✔ look for patterns and connections
- ✔ state my new understanding

Interpret and Analyze Information

Reread the information that you have gathered. Think about what the information means. Dig deeper to figure out why it is important. Check to see if you have enough information to answer your inquiry question.

Evaluate and Draw Conclusions

Look at all the challenges and solutions that you identified. What advice will you provide in your guide? Choose at least three pieces of advice.

When I evaluate and draw conclusions, I will

✔ identify what is important

✔ make a decision or form an opinion to answer my inquiry question

✔ state my conclusion clearly, using evidence

Communicate

Your guide can take the form of a booklet, a media presentation, a video, or a poster. In your guide, describe the three most important challenges that a newcomer to early Canada would face. Give advice about how to overcome those challenges.

Include an introduction and a conclusion. In your guide, use photos, maps, illustrations, charts, lists, or videos.

When I communicate, I will

✔ use words and visuals to present my advice

✔ present the information clearly to help other people understand it

✔ make the information interesting for my audience

Reflect on Your Learning

What did you learn from this investigation? What would you do differently next time?

Glossary

A

Aboriginal peoples: people who have been living in a land from the earliest times; in Canada, Aboriginal peoples are First Nations, Métis, and Inuit

analyzing: taking information apart to help you understand it

B

band council: a group of people who make decisions on how the land is used on a reserve

bilingual country: a country, such as Canada, that has two official languages

C

cause: something that makes an event happen

change: things become different

climate: the usual weather for an area

commerce: buying and selling things for money

consequence: something that happens as a result of an event

continuity: things stay the same

county: a large area with many communities

E

ecopassage: a bridge or tunnel over or under a road, which has been built to protect wildlife

Elders: people who teach the skills, beliefs, and traditions of their community

F

factory: a place where people manufacture goods

forestry: planting, managing, and using trees

fur trade: people trading goods for the fur of animals

G

goods: items that are made for people to use, such as cars, clothing, pots, and vitamins

H

habitants: farmers in New France who worked for the seigneur

I

interpreting: understanding information and putting it in your own words

interrelationships: connections, such as connections between the environment and human activities

isolated: lonely, living apart from others

L

landform features: the natural characteristics of the land, for example, forests and mountains

Loyalists: people who were loyal to Britain. Some of them fought on the British side in a war with the United States

M

manufacturing: the making of goods from materials, such as steel, plastic, and wood

Métis: the children and grandchildren of First Nations women and French men in the fur trade

minerals: materials found in the ground

mining: the removal of minerals from the ground

multiculturalism: people from all cultures who live together in dignity and have respect for one another

N

National Aboriginal Day: a day to honour Aboriginal peoples in Canada

natural resources: things found in nature that are valuable or useful to people

O

official languages: languages that have a special status in a place; for example, English and French in Canada

organic farming: growing food without harmful chemicals

P

patterns: characteristics that are similar and repeat; patterns can be found in nature or created by humans

perspective: how people see things

R

recreation: play and enjoyable activities

regional council: a group of people that make decisions for a region

reserve: land that belongs to First Nations peoples

S

seigneuries: blocks of land divided into long, thin farms in New France

seigneurs: people in charge of big blocks of land in New France called seigneuries

settlers: people who build new communities

significance: importance

slavery: a system in which people are the property of other people

T

transportation: ways that people and things are moved from one place to another

trap: to catch animals

trends: patterns that happen over a period of time

tundra: flat land with no trees, where the ground stays frozen for most of the year

W

wetlands: watery swamps and marshes

wigwam: a type of home made from birchbark, fur, bulrush leaves, and wooden poles

Index

Credits

This page constitutes an extension of the copyright page. We have made every effort to trace the ownership of all copyrighted material and to secure permission from copyright holders. In the event of any question arising as to the use of any material, we will be pleased to make the necessary corrections in future printings. Thanks are due to the following authors, publishers, and agents for permission to use the material indicated.

Text and Images

Bible quotations are from *New Revised Standard Version Bible*, copyright 1989, Division of Christian Education of the National Council of the Churches of Christ in the United States of America. Used by permission. All rights reserved.

2: (top) © Oleksiy Maksymenko/All Canada Photos/Corbis; (middle) © AsianFirecracker/Fotolia; (bottom) © Yvette Cardozo/Alamy. **3:** (top) Paul Kane, Canadian, 1810–1871, *Indian Encampment on Lake Huron*, c. 1845, oil on canvas, Overall: 48.3 x 73.7 cm (19 x 29 in.), ART GALLERY OF ONTARIO, Purchase, 1932, 2121, @2015AGO; (middle) *The Underground Railroad*, 1893 (oil on canvas), Webber, Charles T. (1825–1911)/Cincinnati Art Museum, Ohio, USA/Subscription Fund Purchase/Bridgeman Images. **4:** © travelstock44/Alamy. **5:** StudioIcon/Shutterstock. **7:** ranplett/Getty Images. **12:** Reuters/Frank Gunn. **13:** (top) © Hugh Z/Alamy; (bottom) Toronto Star/Getstock.com. **14:** © Paul Lantz; (top inset) © Dani Friedman/AGE Fotostock; (middle inset) © Paul Lantz; (bottom inset) © Paul Lantz. **15:** (top) © CharlineXia Ontario Canada Collection/Alamy; (top inset) © James Smedley/Alamy; (middle inset) Courtesy of Kim Toffan; (bottom) SF photo/Shutterstock; (bottom inset) Tannis Toohey/GetStock.com. **16:** Jonah Bettio/Nelson Education Ltd. **17:** © Paul Lantz; (inset) Designpics/Inmagine.com. **20:** (bottom): Louie Palu/The Globe and Mail/The Canadian Press; (top) © Paul Lantz. **21:** © Dennis Fast/VWPics/Alamy. **22:** © Yvette Cardozo/Alamy. **23:** © Paul Lantz. **24:** © Paul Lantz. **26:** (top) © Liam Sharp; (bottom) The People of the Kattawapiskak © 2012 National Film Board of Canada. All rights reserved. **27:** (top) Photo by Andrea Waldron, 2012; (bottom) © Paul Lantz. **28:** © Vibe Images/Fotolia.com. **30:** (top) Courtesy of Lianne Linklater; (bottom) © Paul Lantz. **31:** (top) Courtesy of Donna Seary; (bottom) Courtesy of Jean Iron. **33:** © Vibe Images/Fotolia.com. **34:** (top right) © Paul Lantz; (top left) Sylvain Cordier/Getty; (bottom right) Tanya Talaga/Getstock.com; (bottom left) Photo by Denise Lantz. **35:** (top) Jonah Bettio/Nelson Education Ltd.; (left) © Paul Lantz; (right) Designpics/Inmagine.com. **36:** © National Post/Jonathan Kay. **37:** (top) Derek Trask/Getty Images; (bottom) wckiw/Shutterstock. **38:** (top right) © Lisa Thornberg/iStockphoto; (top left) Ryan M. Bolton/Shutterstock; (bottom right) Steve Russell/Getstock.com; (bottom left) Design Pics Inc/Alamy. **39:** (top left) MICHAEL S. LEWIS/National Geographic Creative; (top right) Bill Brooks/Alamy; (bottom left) Les Palenik/Shutterstock; (bottom right) Janet Foster/Getty Images. **41:** (top) Stephen Krasemann/All Canada Photos; (bottom) Don Johnston/All Canada Photos. **43:** Marek Poplawski/Alamy. **44:** Flirt/Alamy. **45:** By P199 (Own work) [CC BY-SA 3.0 (http://creativecommons.org/licenses/by-sa/3.0) or GFDL (http://www.gnu.org/copyleft/fdl.html)], via Wikimedia Commons. **46:** (top) wckiww/Shutterstock; (bottom right) S.J. Krasemann/Getty Images; (bottom left) Parks Canada. **48:** (top) Courtesy of Spencer Gouge; (bottom) Courtesy of Curniss McGoldrick.

49: (top) Courtesy of Donna Mior; (bottom) Courtesy of Dave Paton. 50: (top) © Peter Paradis; (bottom) Greg Taylor/Alamy. 51: (top) FORM Architecture Engineering, Township of Terrace Bay Downtown Revitalization Project; (bottom) Courtesy of the Township of Terrace Bay. 52: wckiww/Shutterstock. 53: Courtesy of Long Point World Biosphere Reserve. 54: (top) Photograph courtesy of Mary Storey; (bottom right) © Oleksiy Maksymenko/All Canada Photos/Corbis; (bottom left) Sun Media; 55: (top) The Canadian Press/Sharon Doucette; (bottom) By Town of Bancroft [CC BY-SA 4.0 (http://creativecommons.org/licenses/by/4.0)], via Flickr. 56: (top) Ken Gillespie Photography/Alamy; (bottom) Fotosearch/AGE Fotostock. 57: (top) Jonah Bettio/Nelson Education Ltd.; (bottom right) wckiww/Shutterstock; (bottom left) © Guoqiang Xue/Alamy. 59: Lissandra Melo/Shutterstock; (inset) © andresr/iStockphoto. 60: (top) foodfolio/Alamy; (bottom left) Toronto Star/Getstock.com; (bottom right) The Canadian Press Images/Maclean's Magazine/Andrew Tolson. 61: (top left) CRAIG GLOVER/The London Free Press/QMI Agency; (top right) © tomeng/iStockphoto; (bottom) Gaertner/Alamy. 63: (top) Courtesy of Dr. Jim Mottin; (bottom) © Fertnig/iStockphoto. 64: © AsianFirecracker/Fotolia. 65: (left) Kathy deWitt/Alamy; (right) Archives/QMI Agency. 66: © andresr/iStockphoto. 67: (top) Sun Media; (bottom) CRAIG GLOVER/The London Free Press/QMI Agency. 68: Tom Wagner/Alamy. 69: Bill Brooks/Alamy. 70: Bill Brooks/Alamy. 71: MaximImages/Alamy. 72: (top) Courtesy of Parmi Takk; (bottom) Courtesy of Brother Tom Liss. 73: (top) Courtesy of Darlene Hayden; (bottom) Courtesy of Evan Winter. 74: SF photo/Shutterstock; (inset) By Permute (Own work) [CC BY-SA 3.0 (http://creativecommons.org/licenses/by-sa/3.0)], via Wikimedia Commons. 75: © Darko Zeljkovic; (inset) anonymous donor; 76: Prisma Bildagentur AG/Alamy. 77: © Nicole Di Cintio. 78: © andresr/iStockphoto. 79: Songquan Deng/Shutterstock. 80: Bernard Weil/GetStock.com. 81: (top) Jonah Bettio/Nelson Education Ltd; (left) Lucas Oleniuk/GetStock.com; (right) © andresr/iStockphoto. 82: Lucy/Shutterstock. 83: (top) Andresr/Shutterstock; (bottom) Darrin Henry/Shutterstock. 84: Jacek Chabraszewski/Shutterstock. 85: Ariel Skelley/Getty. 89: Library and Archives Canada, Acc. No. 1983-47-21. 90: (bottom left) Thomas Davies, *A View of Château-Richer Church near Québec in Canada*, Taken in 1788, 1788 Watercolour over graphite on laid paper, 34.3 x 51.8 cm, National Gallery of Canada, Ottawa, Photo © NGC. 91: (top left) Paul Kane, Canadian, 1810–1871, *Indian Encampment on Lake Huron*, c. 1845, oil on canvas, Overall: 48.3 x 73.7 cm (19 x 29 in.), ART GALLERY OF ONTARIO, Purchase, 1932, 2121, @2015AGO; (bottom) City of Toronto Museums and Heritage Services, A82-28. 92: Jonah Bettio/Nelson Education Ltd. 93: Paul Kane, Canadian, 1810–1871, *Indian Encampment on Lake Huron*, c. 1845, oil on canvas, Overall: 48.3 x 73.7 cm (19 x 29 in.), ART GALLERY OF ONTARIO, Purchase, 1932, 2121, @2015AGO; (inset) © Vikram Raghuvanshi/iStockphoto. 94–95: (background) © CharlineXia Ontario Canada Collection/Alamy. 94: (top) Container with lid, 1900–1925, 20th Century, M973.85.6A, McCord Museum, Montréal; (middle) Marilyn Angel Wynn/Getty Images; (bottom) Rattle, 1865–1900, 19th Century, M12574, McCord Museum, Montréal. 95: (top left) Nativestock.com/Marilyn Angel Wynn/Getty Images; (top right) Moccasin, 1900–1915, 20th Century, M1078.9-10, McCord Museum, Montréal; (bottom left) © Marilyn Angel Wynn/Nativestock Pictures/Corbis; (bottom right) Cooking Pot, 17th Century, M996X.2.480, McCord Museum, Montréal. 97: Keith Beaty/Toronto Star/Getty Images. 101: © Peter Beck/CORBIS. 103: (top) Courtesy of Holy Angels School; (bottom) Glenbow Archives, NA-1406-23. 104: © Vikram Raghuvanshi/iStockphoto. 105: *Indians transporting furs through the Canadian wilderness*, 1858 (oil on canvas), Krieghoff, Cornelius (1815–72)/Hudson Bay Company, Canada/Bridgeman Images. 106: © Dani Friedman/AGE Fotostock. 107: (top) Jonah Bettio/Nelson Education Ltd.; (bottom left) © Brian Summers/AGE Fotostock; (bottom right) © Vikram Raghuvanshi/iStockphoto. 109: (top) Thomas Davies, *A View of Château-Richer Church near Québec in Canada*, Taken in 1788, 1788, Watercolour over graphite on laid paper, 34.3 x 51.8 cm, National Gallery of Canada, Ottawa, Photo © NGC; (bottom) Sergey Novikov/Shutterstock. 113: Thomas Davies, *A View of the Château-Richer, Cape Torment, and Lower End of the Isle of Orleans near Québec*, 1787, Watercolour on laid paper, 35.4 x 52.7 cm, National Gallery of Canada, Ottawa, Photo © NGC. **116:** Sergey Novikov/Shutterstock. **118:** Cornelius Krieghoff, *The Blizzard*, 1857, Oil on canvas, 33.4 x 46.1 cm, National Gallery of Canada, Ottawa, Photo © NGC. **119:** (right) Photo courtesy of Blessed Teresa of Calcutta Catholic Elementary School, Hamilton; (left) Cornelius Krieghoff, *Indian Wigwam in Lower Canada*, 1848, Lithograph with watercolour on wove paper, 43.7 x 57.5 cm; image: 35.5 x 49.5 cm, National Gallery of Canada, Ottawa, Gift of Donald Maclaren, Ottawa, 1990, Photo © NGC. **120:** © david sanger photography/Alamy. **121:** (top) Jonah Bettio/Nelson Education Ltd.; (bottom right) Sergey Novikov/Shutterstock; (bottom left) Mieke Dalle/Getty Images. **123:** (bottom) eurobanks/Shutterstock. **126:** Granger, NYC—All rights reserved. **128:** Garry Black/Getty Images. **129:** (left and right) Village Historique Acadien © 2002. **130:** (top) Hemis/Alamy; (bottom) Stephen Saks/Getty Images. **131:** Library and Archives Canada, e010952204. **132:** eurobanks/Shutterstock. **134:** Paul McKinnon/Shutterstock. **135:** (top) Jonah Bettio/Nelson Education Ltd.; (left) Rick Madonik/GetStock.com; (right) eurobanks/Shutterstock. **137:** (top) Library and Archives Canada, Acc. No. 1938-220-1; (bottom) wavebreakmedia/Shutterstock. **140:** *The Underground Railroad*, 1893 (oil on canvas), Webber, Charles T. (1825-1911)/Cincinnati Art Museum, Ohio, USA/Subscription Fund Purchase/Bridgeman Images. **142:** wavebreakmedia/Shutterstock. **144:** Radius Images/Getty. **145:** Ellis Little Local History Room, Waterloo Public Library. **146:** Colin McConnell/GetStock.com. **147:** (top) Jonah Bettio/Nelson Education Ltd.; (bottom left) Tony Bock/Toronto Star/GetStock.com; (bottom right) wavebreakmedia/Shutterstock. **149:** (top) Library and Archives Canada, Acc. No. 1990-569-22; (bottom) wavebreakmedia/Shutterstock. **150:** Library and Archives Canada, Acc. No. 1970-188-2092 W.H. Coverdale Collection of Canadiana. **151:** City of Toronto Museums and Heritage Services, A82-28. **152:** Library and Archives Canada, Acc. No. 1990-336-3. **154:** City of Toronto Archives, Fonds 1231, Item 96. **155:** City of Toronto Museums and Heritage Services, 1978.41.51. **157:** (top) Courtesy of Thomas D'Arcy McGee School. **158:** wavebreakmedia/Shutterstock. **160:** © Gregory Holmgren/Alamy. **161:** (top) Jonah Bettio/Nelson Education Ltd.; (bottom right) wavebreakmedia/Shutterstock; (bottom left) Colin McConnell/The Canadian Press. **162:** Colin McConnell/Getstock.com. **163:** Jupiterimages/Thinkstock. **164:** petrograd99/Thinkstock. **165:** Chris Hendrickson/Masterfile.

Sources

10: St John Paul II, *On Human* Work. **109:** Encyclical Letter Caritas In Veritate of the Supreme Pontiff Benedict XVI to the Bishops, Priests and Deacons, Men and Women Religious, The Lay, Faithful, and All People of Good Will on Integral Human Development In Charity and Truth from The Vatican at http://www.vatican.va/holy_father/benedict_xvi/encyclicals/documents/hf_ben-xvi_enc_20090629_caritas-in-veritate_en.html#_edn127. **149:** Visit at the Homeless Shelter "Dono Di Maria": Meeting With the Missionaries of Charity, Address of Pope Francis, Tuesday, 21 May 2013 found at https://w2.vatican.va/content/francesco/en/speeches/2013/may/documents/papa-francesco_20130521_dono-di-maria.html.

St. Francis Xavier Elementary School
111 Bartley Bull Parkway
Brampton, Ontario
L6W 2J8